Using Positive Psychology Enhance Student Achievem

Positive psychology, properly understood and applied, offers a tremendous opportunity for improving student and teacher experiences and the overall success of any school. The connection between education and happiness is recognised to be mutually reinforcing; education helps students to be happy and happy students gain more from education. Research has confirmed what educators have long known – that happy students typically achieve more in the classroom and exam room than unhappy students and are more energetic, persistent, creative and better able to get on with others.

Using Positive Psychology to Enhance Student Achievement is unique in translating a complex literature written by academic psychologists into a highly practical resource. The activities have been designed to provide a creative and engaging way of enabling students to discover their strengths both in terms of their cognitive abilities and 'virtues', i.e. character strengths.

Throughout the programme, students are introduced to the key insights of positive psychology:

- the importance of being connected to others
- character training and metacognitive strategies
- positive rather than reactive thinking and habits
- developing the skills essential for building optimism and resilience
- recognising and combating negative thoughts
- understanding that there are certain ways of thinking that can make their lives better.

Easy-to-deliver sessions with comprehensive facilitator instructions and activity resources are provided. All lessons are interactive and based on group discussions and role play to ensure that students learn more about themselves and others. Students are encouraged to practise skills and ideas that are discussed during the sessions in their everyday lives with home practise in the form of 'take away' activities as a core element of the programme.

This unique resource will be of real relevance and benefit to both staff and students at upper primary and lower secondary levels and will give students the tools they need to achieve their full potential.

Tina Rae is a Consultant Educational Psychologist and has a wealth of experience in working therapeutically with children and young people and their parents/carers. She is a registered member of the HCPC (Health and Care Professions Council) and a member of the British Psychological Society. She is currently working as a consultant EP and as an academic and professional tutor on the doctoral training course for Educational Psychologists in the department of Psychology at the University of East London.

Ruth MacConville is Head of SEN Service, London Borough of Ealing and author of a variety of books on resilience, friendship skills and well-being. She has been an invited speaker and workshop leader at a variety of national and local conferences and regularly delivers training sessions to mainstream and special schools on a variety of topics.

Using Positive Psychology to Enhance Student Achievement

A schools-based programme for character education

Tina Rae and Ruth MacConville

 Routledge
Taylor & Francis Group

LONDON AND NEW YORK

First published 2015
by Routledge
2 Park Square, Milton Park, Abingdon, Oxon OX14 4RN

Simultaneously published in the USA and Canada
by Routledge
711 Third Avenue, New York, NY 10017

Routledge is an imprint of the Taylor & Francis Group, an informa business

British Library Cataloguing in Publication Data
A catalogue record for this book is available from the British Library

Library of Congress Cataloging-in-Publication Data
Rae, Tina, author.
Using positive psychology to enhance student achievement : achievement using the hidden
    power of character / Tina Rae and Ruth MacConville.
        pages cm
    Includes bibliographical references and index.
    1. Academic achievement—Psychological aspects.   2. Educational psychology.   3. Positive
psychology.   4. Moral education.   5. Character—Study and teaching.   I. MacConville, Ruth,
author.   II. Title.
    LB1062.6.R34 2014
    370.15—dc23
    2014020170

ISBN: 978-1-138-79153-4 (hbk)
ISBN: 978-1-138-79154-1 (pbk)
ISBN: 978-1-315-76274-6 (ebk)

Typeset in Helvetica
by Apex CoVantage, LLC

Printed and bound by CPI Group (UK) Ltd, Croydon, CR0 4YY

Contents

Section 1
Introduction

Since the publication of *Building Happiness, Resilience and Motivation in Adolescents: A Positive Psychology Curriculum for Well-Being* (MacConville and Rae 2012), there has been an increasing demand for practical resources which enable practitioners to use the findings of positive psychology in their day-to-day practise. This has, in part, been due to the wealth of recent research that highlights the inextricable link between an individual's well-being and their capacity to achieve. Over the past few years dedicated researchers have explored the patterns of thinking, feeling and relating that create human success. It is now recognised that well-being is not a stand-alone feature of individuals; rather it is inextricably linked to that individual's ability to flourish and achieve. The connection between education and happiness is now firmly established as being mutually reinforcing; education helps individuals to be happy and happy people gain more from education. A powerful body of research by positive psychologist Barbara Frederikson (2009) confirms what educators have long known that happy students typically learn and perform better in the classroom than unhappy students. They are more energetic, persistent, focused, creative and better able to get on with their peers and staff. Human flourishing enhances learning the traditional goal of education.

This book is designed to be used with students in the secondary phase. Our previous book provided an introduction to the twenty-four character strengths identified by Christopher Peterson and Martin Seligman (2004), and the emphasis was very much on understanding each of the character strengths and exploring how they show up and can be used in our daily lives. This book continues to employ a strengths approach to enabling students to flourish and explores what Paul Tough (2012) calls 'the hidden power of character'. It emphasises the process by which character strengths can be identified and strengthened in our daily lives and draws on recent research on how to re-programme our daily habits.

The focus in this resource is on what practitioners can do to enable young people to develop their strengths as a way of shaping their understanding of how to build productive habits, do better goal setting, re-engineer the way that they think about mistakes and failure and learn how to recognise, 'savour' and celebrate success. Angela Duckworth (quoted in Seligman 2011, p. 103) explains:

> The problem, I think, is not only the schools but also the students themselves. Here's why: learning is hard. True, learning is fun, exhilarating,

and gratifying – but it is also often daunting, exhausting, and sometimes discouraging. By and large, students who no longer want to learn, who don't think they can learn, and who don't see any point in learning simply won't – no matter how wonderful the school or teacher. . . . To help low performing but intelligent students, educators must first recognise that character is at least as important as intellect.

Positive psychologists agree that enabling young people to develop and use their character strengths is what enables them to move forward with purpose and enthusiasm. Character strengths also have the potential to enable young people to manage uncertain times and deal with the pressures that they are under from the digital world with its promise of constant connectedness, eternal beauty and unlimited success. Since there is a considerable overlap between character strengths and resilience and these skills can be taught and contribute significantly to life success, they are a crucial part of education in its widest sense. In an essay on fostering resilience Sebastian Kraemer (1999) of London's Tavistock Clinic, writes:

> In a world in which individuality is acknowledged, even celebrated, resilience is best understood as the experience of agency: that what you do or say makes a difference, that it is worthwhile making plans for your life, that you are not simply a helpless victim of forces entirely beyond your control.

The most fundamental way in which educators who support this process can do this is by demonstrating a positive outlook on life and by committing ourselves to discovering our own strengths and the strengths in others.

Using this book

This book is written in four parts. Following this opening, the next section contains an introduction to positive psychology and explores how the power of habit and qualities such as perseverance, conscientiousness optimism and self-control are essential components of success. The second part of the book contains a PowerPoint presentation that can be used to introduce the programme to staff. The third part contains the resources that form the programmes. The book ends with information for parents, suggestions for further reading and a list of useful websites.

About the programmes

The programmes that are presented in this book are complete, ready-to-use sets of resources. They introduce the core elements of positive psychology and convey them in a clear and practical way. Devised with the aim of provoking thoughtful discussions, engaging activities, strength-discovering exercises and confidence boosting fun, the practical activities in the programmes aim to enable students how to:

- recognise their character strengths
- use them in new ways
- build healthy and happy habits
- make value-based decisions.

The programmes comprise a wide range of activities that practitioners can use with students in the secondary phase to stimulate the recognition and development of their character strengths and healthy habit formation. They aim to enable students to recognise the practical skills that they can use to make their lives go better. The activities are intended to be interactive and supported by group discussions and partner work to ensure that students learn more about themselves and others. The programmes are intended to be delivered with a sense of fun to engage and inspire all learners.

This book does not claim to be an exhaustive account of positive psychology. It is designed to be a practical and informed starting point for practitioners who recognise the importance of building strengths-based partnerships with young people through a taught programme and through the development of a positive school environment which is congruent with the values that the programme promotes.

Our vision in writing this book is that positive psychology and strengths-based partnerships with young people should become essential tools for practitioners because we believe that they have the capacity to focus our beliefs and practise on positive outcomes, on what is going well rather than what has gone wrong, what can be done rather than what cannot be done and because they encourage us to celebrate strengths in ourselves and others.

Positive psychology

Positive psychology is a relatively new field of study that is concerned with subjective well-being, the technical term for happiness and how individuals can flourish. It was introduced in 1998 by psychologist Martin Seligman, when he was elected to be president of the American Psychological Association. During his presidential address, Seligman (who is recognized as a world authority on depression, pessimism and learned helplessness) made the case that psychology was good, but not good enough, because it had neglected the study and application of the things that make life worth living. Seligman emphasised that the time had come for a positive psychology that would redress this imbalance and focus research on what was right with people, including happiness, well-being and human strengths. Seligman argued that alongside the work of studying mental illness, psychologists should also study human well-being, character strengths and human potential and look at talented and flourishing individuals as well as those who are struggling. A recurring theme of this new science is that using our strengths taps into the core of who we are as human beings and how we can make our greatest contribution. Jenny Fox Eades (2008), Programme Director for Schools and Young People at the not-for-profit Centre for Applied Positive Psychology (CAPP), explains that positive psychology studies areas like contentment, hope, optimism, pleasure and engagement. It focuses on positive traits such as love, courage and creativity and virtues like citizenship, tolerance and responsibility.

Average is not good enough

Alex Linley (2008), positive psychologist, social entrepreneur and founder of CAPP, writes about the importance of avoiding the 'curse of mediocrity'. He argues that average isn't good enough. Linley explains that when people are asked how they would rate themselves on a variety of positive characteristics, almost everyone rates themselves as being above average, which of course, by definition, can't be true but it does illustrate the point that we simply don't want to be average – 'we all want to be better than average. We want to be A+' (p. 1). Positive psychologists explore the lives of outstanding individuals and asks how it is that they function so well. They also look at 'average' people and ask what is working well and what is getting better.

Positive psychology brings scientific rigour and experiment to the field of human flourishing and provides a framework that draws together previously unconnected ideas. It has its roots in the work of William James in the late nineteenth century and humanistic psychology in the mid-twentieth century as well as in the work of ancient philosophers such as Aristotle and Plato. Seligman (2011) has recently challenged the generally accepted view that positive psychology is primarily about seeking happiness and suggests that we have lost contact with the spiritual and philosophical traditions of happiness and have settled for a weaker, more selfish version which is about enjoyment, pleasure and the avoidance of pain and suffering.

The aim of positive psychology then is to describe rather than prescribe how we can enable individuals to flourish and realise the highest levels of their potential. Led by the pioneering work of Martin Seligman, many psychologists have turned their attention to studying patterns of thinking, feeling and relating that facilitate human success and flourishing; thus there is now a body of knowledge verified by science that can inform us how to live a fulfilling life. It emphasises the value of relationships, meaning and engagement and plays down the importance of consumerism. Happiness or flourishing in Western societies has proved to be only weakly affected by demographic characteristics such as wealth and material possessions.

Subjective well-being (the technical term for happiness), then, is important not just because it feels good but because it creates better commerce with the world. It enables us to be healthier, harder working and more involved with family, friends and the community. There is increasing evidence that well-being is a powerful preventative and remedial 'medicine' as well as something that enables us to flourish.

At the beginning of the last decade very few people had heard of the term 'positive psychology'; now its effects can be felt across the nation. For most of us here in the UK, the biggest visible effect has been a stream of headlines and features devoted to this new science. Positive psychology has proved itself much more media-friendly than traditional psychology and its studies into weakness, pathology and mental illness. A slew of sunny books have lured us with promises that we, too, can be happier – and here's the science to prove it. From BBC programmes investigating the happiness quotient of entire towns such as the television documentary in 2004, *Making Slough Happy*, to parliamentary groups investigating the nation's well-being we are gradually beginning to embrace the idea that we can master our positive emotions, and recognise success not just by what we earn, what we do or where we live but by our feelings of satisfaction and authenticity. Recent findings from the first survey carried out by the Office for National Statistics as part of a £2 million 'happiness index', set up by prime minister, David Cameron, suggest that despite the current economic doom-and-gloom, 76 per cent of people rated themselves happy and consider that the things that they do in life are worthwhile. Mark Williamson, founder of the Action for Happiness campaign (www.actionforhappiness.org), comments that the overall figures from the survey suggest that despite current economic wobbles, we're actually resilient here in the UK, thus suggesting that not all happiness comes down to our bank balance or how much stuff we own.

One of the criticisms often made about positive psychology is that it's all about happiness. In his latest book *Flourish: A new understanding of happiness and well-being and how to achieve them*, Martin Seligman (2011) explains that he has now come to detest the 'H word', a term which he considers has now been so overused that it has become almost meaningless. Seligman suggests that the modern ear now immediately hears 'happy' to only mean pleasure, enjoyment and good cheer and is therefore not a topic that is worthy of academic, scientific endeavour. Seligman writes that he now prefers to use the term 'flourishing', which he believes captures the values which are similar to what major spiritual traditions have talked about for centuries far more accurately. In this sense, positive psychology emphases are as old as the Talmud, the New Testament and the Koran. Like many ancient philosophies and spiritual traditions, an important idea of this new science is that seeking happiness for its own sake does not lead to long-term happiness. To understand this we have to appreciate the difference between the happiness that you feel from experiencing pleasure in the moment and the happiness we gain from meaning and purpose in our lives, fulfilling our potential and a feeling that we are part of something bigger than ourselves. We experience short-lived pleasure when we satisfy basic needs such as hunger and bodily comfort. We flourish, on the other hand, when we stretch ourselves, when we break through some of our self-imposed limits and experience personal growth and joy.

Three ascending levels of happiness

Dan Nettle (2005), reader in psychology at the University of Newcastle, describes three ascending levels of happiness in his book, *Happiness: The science behind your smile.*

> Level 1: The most immediate and direct state of happiness involves transient feelings like joy or pleasure that are attained. There is not much thinking involved beyond the recognition that the desired thing has happened.
>
> Level 2: When people say that they are happy with their lives, they usually don't mean that they are experiencing pleasure in their lives all the time. Rather they mean that on reflection, on the balance sheet of pleasure and pain the balance is reasonably positive over the long-term. This level of happiness is not so much concerned with pleasure and feelings as with judgements about the balance of feelings and can be summed up by terms such as contentment and life satisfaction.
>
> Level 3: This state cannot be easily measured as it involves a broader sense of happiness and perhaps can most accurately summed up by Aristotle's ideal of the good life called 'eudaimonia' which refers to a lives in which individuals flourish and fulfil their true potential.

Seligman (2011) believes then that the term 'flourishing' is far more in touch with the Aristotle's view of happiness (Barnes, 1984). Aristotle claimed that a major purpose in life was to experience happiness and that this is attained through living a virtuous life and focusing on strengths instead of weaknesses. Although the science of positive psychology is relatively new, its emphasis on 'excellence of activity' is firmly documented in every culture of the last 3,000 years.

PERMA: a new theory of well-being

Seligman's (2011) revised theory of well-being 'PERMA' consists of five separate elements:

1. Positive emotion
2. Engagement
3. Relationships
4. Meaning
5. Accomplishment

> **P**ositive emotion: The experience of positive mood and experiences.
>
> **E**ngagement (or 'flow', as it is usually called): Refers to the well-being you get from being totally absorbed in the task in hand, so much so that you lose track of time and feel at one with what you are doing.
>
> **R**elationships: Studies suggest that healthy, caring and supportive interpersonal connections are essential to our well-being throughout life.

Meaning: Provides both a stable foundation and a sense of direction in life. Pursuing meaningful activities has been found to be more strongly related to well-being than pursuing pleasurable ones.

Accomplishment: Is the most recent psychological component in Seligman's well-being model. It includes everything from achievement, success and mastery at the highest level possible to progress towards goals and competence.

Positive education

Positive education is the incorporation of these five elements of well-being into the life and work of schools. Seligman (2011, p. 78) writes:

> The schooling of children has, for more than a century, paved the boulevard towards adult work. I am all for success, literacy, perseverance, and discipline, but I want you to imagine that schools could, without compromising either, teach both the skills of well-being and the skills of achievement. I want you to imagine positive education.

In a recent article 'Think Tank, New Ideas for the 21st Century', Anthony Seldon (2011), master of Wellington College in Berkshire, made a similar plea:

> Exams are, of course, essential. They allow us to measure the progress of students and school performance. But they are not the whole purpose of schools. The objective that now needs to be prioritised is character building. . . . The point that many in our education department are missing is that an emphasis on the development of character will only improve exam performance at school and university: it will not turn out responsible and thoughtful citizens. . . . The best state schools are already showing the way, by achieving top academic results and offering character education and real enrichment outside the classroom . . . and emphasising the development of good personality and self-control.

The point that many educators are missing, suggests Seligman (2011), is that schools need not be obsessed with exams to be successful. The 'exam factory' mentality is robbing teachers of their professionalism and pupils of curiosity and delight in learning. Seligman writes that if we want to maximise the achievement of children, we need to promote self-discipline which he describes as 'the queen of all the virtues, the strength that enables the rest of the strengths'. In her ground-breaking self-control versus IQ study in *Psychological Science* in 2005, psychologist Angela Duckworth (Duckworth and Seligman 2005) demonstrated that self-control is often a more reliable predictor of students' university success than their IQ. Duckworth subsequently began to suspect that self-control wasn't exactly the driver of success that she was looking for and, with Christopher Peterson, developed a test to measure GRIT. According to Seligman (2011), GRIT is a never-yielding form of self-discipline. Very high effort is caused by a personality characteristic of extreme persistence. The more GRIT you have, the more time you spend on the task, and all those hours don't just add to whatever innate skill you have; they multiply your progress to the goal. Duckworth et al. (2007) developed a test to measure GRIT, which she called the GRIT Scale. It is a deceptively simple test, available in the public domain. It consists of 12 brief statements on which respondents must evaluate themselves and then score themselves on a five-point scale. The test takes about three minutes to complete and relies entirely on self report. When Duckworth and Peterson took the GRIT scale out into the field, they found it was extremely predictive of success.

Seligman (2011, p. 125) writes:

> Higher human accomplishment is one of the four components of flourishing and yet another reason that will and character are indispensable objects of the science of positive psychology. My hope (actually, my prediction) is that this decade will see major discoveries in how to increase GRIT and self-control.

Professor Howard Gardner (2011) of Harvard University has shown conclusively that IQ is only one of several intelligences that we possess. If schools do not develop all them, including creativity, personal and moral intelligence, these qualities may remain dormant for life. Seligman has emphasized that it is possible for schools to achieve top academic results and teach well-being and character building and that this can be accomplished through what he terms 'Positive Education'.

Excellence of activity

Aristotle claimed that a virtue or character strength is developed through action: brave people became brave by doing brave things. At the basis of positive education then is the concept of 'excellence of activity' and the recognition that when you know how to do something well and act on this, it can bring engagement and meaning in your life and it can enable an individual to achieve success and mastery at the highest level. It follows that the more things that you know how to do well, the more avenues you will have for both mastery and positive growth. The work of Jenny Fox Eades (2008) is concerned with building strength-based schools in the South Leys Cluster in Scunthorpe, North East Lincolnshire. Fox Eades writes that being part of a school where the focus is primarily on strengths not weaknesses, and where staff and students aim not at just being 'OK' but being the best they can be can is an uplifting experience for all concerned. At the basis then of positive education is the need to ensure that in schools all our relationships are characterised by healthy, caring and supportive interpersonal connections with others. Roy Baumeister (2005, p.109) summarizes the evidence: 'Whether someone has a network of good relationships or is alone in the world is a much stronger predictor of happiness than any other objective predictor.'

Social contagion: spiral up or spiral down

Social contagion is the term used by positive psychologists for moods spreading from person to person. We are, [it seems,] physically constructed to make this possible. Daniel Goleman (2007) in *Social Intelligence* writes about our mirror neurons that fire in response to observing behaviour or emotions in others. We pick up emotions from others not just because we see and interpret them rationally, but also because we experience them directly in the firing of our mirror neurons. Social contagion can be in either positive or negative directions. (Britton 2008, pp. 1–2)

Optimism and negativity can both spread rapidly through groups. Fox Eades (2008) writes that creating environments that support others to grow by focusing on their strengths enables both students and colleagues to find new ways of relating to each other in positive and productive ways.

Positive psychologists emphasise the importance of increasing the probability that the moods that spread around and through us are positive rather than negative and suggests that this relies on paying conscious attention to the connections (i.e., 'brief exchanges rather than deep relationships' Britton [2008, pp. 1–2]) that we have with others throughout the day. In her book *Energize your Workplace* Jane Dutton (2003, p. 2) in suggests that:

any point of contact with another person can potentially be a high-quality connection. One conversation, one e-mail exchange, one moment of connecting in a meeting can infuse both participants with a greater sense of vitality, giving them a bounce in their steps and a greater capacity to act.

High-quality connections boost positive mood, increase the likelihood that people will help each other, increase the energy that individuals have for persisting at tasks, all of which contribute to improved task performance.

As we will explore later, increasing our well-being is inextricably linked to cultivating the right habits. Many different activities have been tested by psychologists and some have been shown to reliably improve how we feel from day to day. These include boosting our social connections.

Dutton (2003) makes the following practical suggestions, based on her own experience, for developing habits that are built around paying attention to the connections that we have with others throughout the day.

Let your good moods show. When I'm feeling happy, I notice that people I pass smile back at me. Presumably their motor neurons are giving them a quick taste of the good feelings that I am experiencing.

Pay attention to the quality of your connections with others and look to behave in ways that create high-quality connections. Little actions such as advocating for them and accommodating their preferences build trust, show respectful engagement and enable others to do their tasks effectively. (Britton 2008, pp. 1–2)

- Responding enthusiastically to another's good news is a further suggestion. Shelley Gable et al. (2004) calls this 'active constructive responding', and her work suggests that this is far more important to building positive connections than how we communicate with others during bad times.
- Make a conscious effort not to join in with another's unhappiness unless there's something constructive that you can contribute. This means that when a colleague is miserable actively resist joining in the gloom. Don't deny the other person's unhappiness but stay detached from the emotions.
- Protect yourself from corrosive connections, i.e., exchanges that make you feel diminished. It helps to name the experience and detach yourself for responsibility for it: it's not about you but about the other person's social ineptness.
- Avoid complaining. Getting together with another person or a group to complain is a recipe for a downward spiral. Someone is bound to mention some other negative aspect you hadn't thought of yet. Dr Ian Smith (2010) writes that one of the greatest threats to a productive workplace is what he calls 'the viral infection of negativity' that spreads quietly and festers for some time before it starts causing harm. We therefore have to learn to keep negativity in check.

Mindful habits

Psychologist and author Jeremy Dean (2013) explains in relation to cultivating happiness-boosting habits that 'unfortunately there's rather a large fly in the ointment. That fly is habituation'. Habituation means that we adapt to positive experiences more quickly than negative ones. This means that we lose the pleasure from good habits more quickly than the pain from bad ones. One way suggests Dean that we can deal with our automatic adaptation to pleasure is by varying our habits rather than repeating them in exactly the same way over and over again. This could mean, for example, making a conscious effort to respond more consciously to the question 'how are you?' (rather than saying 'Fine' every time). Introducing conscious variations in some of our habits can be effective in reducing the effects of habituation. Although Dean explains that this idea stretches the formal definition of a habit which involves the same behaviour or thought in the same situation, for 'happy' habits we need an 'automatic initiation of the behaviour, but then a mindful continuously way of carrying it out. A new type of hybrid habit; a mindful habit'.

Mirrored pain

We should however not set out to protect ourselves from what is termed 'mirrored' pain. Dan Goleman (2007, p. 55) writes:

Scientific observations point to a response system that is hard-wired in the human brain – no doubt involving instantly mirror neurons that acts when we someone else suffering, making us instantly feel with them. The more we feel with them, the more we want to help them.

This source of compassionate behaviour, is part of what makes us fully human. But we need to moderate our automatic responses when there is no constructive action we can take.

Our ability to mirror other's experiences in our own brains leaves us open to social contagion in either upward or downward spirals. With conscious effort, we can raise the probability that we experience upward rather than downward spirals. (Britton 2008, pp. 1–2)

This is important in the workplace because our moods contribute to the effectiveness of our practise.

Although both positive and negative thinking are important in the right situation, all too often suggests Martin Seligman (2011, p. 80) schools emphasise critical thinking and following orders rather than creative thinking and learning new stuff with the result that many children rank the appeal of going to school just slightly above going to the dentist. 'In the modern world' writes Seligman, 'I believe that we have finally arrived at an era in which more creative thinking, less rote following of orders and yes – even more enjoyment will succeed better'.

It is becoming increasingly apparent that we are living in uncertain times and security is an illusion. Our schools, therefore need to transform into places that give children the tools that they will need to design their futures. We cannot therefore simply prepare young people for lives of security we must also instil in them a sense of hope and the ability to be resilient in the face of uncertainty. They will also need the resources of optimism, collaboration, creativity, emotional intelligence and motivation.

Knowledge Is Power Program (KIPP)

The charter schools in America, especially those in the Knowledge is Power Program (KIPP), have been influential in demonstrating the success of establishing what they term 'character education' in their schools. In his book *How Children Succeed: Grit, Curiosity and the Hidden Power of Character*, Paul Tough (2012) describes how David Levin, the programme's co-founder, had long been concerned by the dropout rates at university of students from the poorest backgrounds at KIPP schools. In 1999, 38 black, Hispanic teenagers, almost all from low-income families, had been recruited four years earlier from their fourth-grade classrooms by Levin with the promise that if they enrolled in his new middle school, he would transform them from 'typical underperforming Bronx-public-school students into college-bound scholars' (Tough 2012, p. 49). In their four years at KIPP these students experienced an immersive style of schooling combining long days of high-intensity classroom instruction with an elaborate programme of attitude adjustment and behaviour modification. Levin's approach seemed to work and in 1999 the students of KIPP Academy earned the highest scores on any school in the

Bronx and the fifth highest in the whole of New York City. Those unprecedented high scores at that time for an open-admission school in a poor neighbourhood helped convince Doris and Donald Fisher, the founders of Gap, to put millions of philanthropic dollars behind an effort to turn KIPP into a national network. That project has led to the creation of more than a hundred new KIPP schools over the past decade.

Subsequent research showed, however, that only a third of students graduating from KIPP completed a four-year university course. Tough (2012) writes that it was painful for Levin to watch those first students struggle through their college experience and as the dropout reports rolled in, Levin noticed that the students who persisted at college were not necessarily the students who had excelled academically at KIPP but those who possessed character strengths such as resilience, tenacity, optimism and social agility.

Since KIPP's beginnings, Levin and KIPP's co-founder, Michael Feinberg, had, in fact, explicitly set out to provide students with lessons in character as well as academics. They filled the walls with slogans such as 'Work hard', 'Be nice', and 'There are no shortcuts'; and they had also promoted team work, empathy and perseverance. What Levin and Feinberg came to realise was missing, however, was the absence of an established structure, or curriculum for teaching character or even talking about it. This meant that each year, discussions at KIPP schools would start from scratch with staff debating which values and behaviours they were trying to nurture in their students and why and how?

Levin and Feinberg eventually met Martin Seligman in Philadelphia and were introduced to the book that he had just finished with Christopher Peterson (2004), *Character Strengths and Virtues: A Handbook and Classification*. To Levin and Feinberg, this 800-page volume represented 'a science of good character'.

Character, writes Tough (2012), is one of those words that 'can complicate any conversation because it can mean different things to different people' (p. 58). Although for many of us character refers to a core set of attributes that defines one's essence something innate and unchanging, Tough writes that Peterson and Seligman (2004) defined character in a very different way, as a set of abilities or strengths that are very much changeable. They are skills that you can learn, practise and teach. What convinced Levin and Feinberg of the value of Peterson and Seligman's approach was that it focused not on morality or ethics but on personal growth and achievement.

Building a strength's approach

Studying strengths is central to positive psychology just as studying disorder and dysfunction is central to traditional psychology. Christopher Peterson and Martin Seligman (2004) set out to standardise the concepts of virtue and strengths. They looked across three thousand years of cultures and religions and identified what they considered were the core virtues that can be found in all of them. Faced with hundreds of character strengths they applied several criteria in order to distil the key strengths that they believed to be universal.

This process resulted in the identification of six universal virtues: wisdom, courage, love, justice, temperance and transcendence. We achieve these virtues through our strengths of character. Twenty-four strengths were defined and accepted as the strengths that allow us to achieve these virtues. The 24 character strengths organised into the six universal virtues are listed below.

Values in action: character strengths

1. **Wisdom and knowledge**: Strengths which are all about learning and using new knowledge:
   - Creativity: Thinking of new and interesting ways to do things
   - Curiosity: Taking an interest in what is going on in the world and wanting to find out about new things
   - Judgement: Thinking things through carefully before making up your mind, weighing up all the evidence carefully, being able to change your mind when you get new information
   - Love of learning: Learning new skills and information and enjoying finding out more about the things that you already know
   - Perspective: Being wise and looking at the world in a way that makes sense, being able to give others good advice
2. **Courage**: Emotional strengths and being able to overcome difficulties and reach one's goal:
   - Bravery: Speaking up for what is right, not running away when things get difficult
   - Perseverance: Finishing what you start, keeping going even if things are difficult, enjoying finishing tasks
   - Authenticity: Speaking the truth, being genuine and true to yourself
   - Integrity: Taking responsibility for your feelings and actions and not blaming somebody else when things go wrong
3. **Love**: Interpersonal strengths looking out and being a being a friend to others:
   - Intimacy: Enjoying being close to people
   - Kindness: Helping others and taking care of them
   - Social intelligence: Understanding what makes other people tick, knowing how to fit in and behave in lots of different situations
4. **Justice**: Dealing fairly with people:
   - Teamwork: Working well as a member of a team, being loyal to the group, doing your share
   - Fairness: Treating all people fairly and giving everybody a fair chance

- Leadership: Encouraging your team or group to get things done, organising activities and making sure that they happen
5. **Temperance**: Not overdoing things:
   - Forgiveness: Forgiving those who have done wrong, giving people a second chance
   - Modesty: Not 'bigging' yourself up, not seeking the spotlight, not thinking that you are more special than you are
   - Prudence: Making careful choices, not taking big risks, not saying or doing things that you will later regret
   - Self-control: Controlling your behaviour, not being too emotional, not eating too much
6. **Transcendence**: Strengths that make connections to the universe and provide meaning in life:
   - Awe: Noticing and appreciating beauty and things done well, i.e., skills and talents
   - Gratitude: Being aware of and thankful for the good things that happen to you; taking time to say thank you.
   - Hope: Expecting the best in the future and working towards it, believing that a good future is something that can be built
   - Playfulness: Liking to laugh and play; bringing smiles to other people, sharing a joke and a laugh
   - Spirituality: Having beliefs about the meaning of the universe and about life that shape one's behaviour and provide comfort.

(adapted from Peterson and Seligman 2004)

Identify your strengths

To find your character strengths log onto www.authentichappiness.com, and take the VIA (values in action) signature strengths questionnaire.[1]

According to Seligman and Peterson, the value of these 24 character strengths does not come from their relationship to any particular system of ethics but from their practical benefits – what an individual can actually gain by possessing and expressing them. Peterson and Seligman believed that cultivating these strengths represented a reliable path to 'the good life', a life that is not just happy but also meaningful and fulfilling. Character strengths can function as a substitute for the social safety net, i.e., the support from their families, and culture and ease that individuals from supportive backgrounds have that protects them from the negative consequences of social detours, mistakes and bad decisions. If you don't have the safety net that comes from a supportive background (and many children and young people from low-income families don't), you need to compensate in another way. To succeed you need more grit, more social intelligence and more self-control.

Developing that strength takes a lot of work. Character strengths, believed Seligman and Peterson, could provide the compensation that an individual requires in order to succeed (Tough 2012, p. 102).

Character strengths are simple habits

William James, the American philosopher and psychologist, believed that the traits we call virtues or character strengths are no more or less than simple habits and that it is the responsibility of education to 'chaperone' the formation of habits:

> First, we must make automatic and habitual as early as possible, as many useful actions as we can and guard against the growing into ways that are likely to be disadvantageous to us, as we should guard against the plague. The more details of our daily life that we can hand over to the effortless custody of automatism, the more our higher powers of mind will be set free for their own proper work. There is no more miserable human being than one in whom nothing is habitual but indecision.
> *(William James 1980, Habit, public library, public domain)*

In the tradition of William James, Martin Seligman and his colleague Angela Duckworth have explored ways to ensure that students understand the importance of developing good habits, i.e., that they have made it their default position to do the 'good' thing meaning the more socially acceptable or chosen the long-term–benefit enhancing option.

One of the first steps Levine and Feinberg took to embed character education in their schools following their encounter with Martin Seligman was to introduce SLANT (which is basically a behaviour-modification system) into all their schools. SLANT is a very practical set of classroom habits that enable students to code-switch and recognise and accurately perform every time, without fail, the professional behaviours appropriate to the classroom as opposed to the street. SLANT stands for:

Sit up
Listen
Ask questions
Nod
Track the speaker with your eyes.

As Tough (2012, p. 89) suggests, the implicit message conveyed to students by SLANT was the importance of knowing how to code-switch. Tom Brunzell, Dean of the KIPP Infinity Middle School, explains:

> It is okay to be street on the street for example but if you're in a museum or a college interview or a nice restaurant, you need to know exactly how to act, or you're going to miss out on important opportunities. . . .

At KIPP we are teaching the professional code of behaviour, the college code of behaviour and we have to teach that every minute of the day.

Will power

At the core, then, of the character education is strong focus on an all important habit: will power. A 2005 study by Angela Duckworth and Martin Seligman analysed 164 eighth-grade students, measuring their IQs and other factors, including how much will power the students demonstrated as measured by tests of their self-discipline. Students who showed high levels of will power were more likely to earn higher grades, had fewer absences and spent less time watching television and more hours on homework. The researchers concluded that:

> Highly disciplined adolescents outperformed their more impulsive peers on every academic-performance variable. . . . Self discipline also predicted which students would improve their grades over the course of an academic year, whereas IQ did not. . . . Self-discipline has a bigger effect on academic performance than does intellectual talent. (p. 942)

Studies suggest then that the best way to strengthen will-power and give students advantages in their education and in their lives is to make will-power into a habit. This happens when we learn to choose a certain behaviour in advance and then follow that routine without deviation when an inflection point or challenge occurs.

In his book *The Social Animal: How Success Happens,* David Brooks (2011, p.157) describes the experiences of Erica, a young tennis player who has constructed a series of rituals to deal with her anger and times when her 'composure slipped':

> She would think about her anger and would say to herself, 'This is not who I am. This is an experience that is happening within me.' She imagined a grassy field. On one side was the angry dog of her anger. But on the other was the tennis player who had won her last five matches. She would imaging herself wandering away from the dog and over to the tennis player.

Brooks explains that Erica was trying to establish the right distance between herself and the world. She was reminding herself that she had a say in triggering which inner self would dominate her behaviour. All she had to do was focus her attention on one internal character rather than another. The act of focusing attention requires an immense display of mental force. William James was among the first to understand the stakes involved in this sorts of decisions: 'efforts of attention is thus the essential phenomenon of the will' (Brooks 2011, p. 157). Brooks concludes that 'those who have habits and strategies to control their attention can control their lives' (p. 157).

Angela Duckworth (quoted in Duhigg 2012, p. 131) observes: 'Sometimes it looks like people with great self-control aren't working hard – but that's because they've made it automatic. Their will power occurs without them having to think about it.'

Cognitive behavioural therapy

Cognitive Behavioural Therapy (CBT) provides the theoretical underpinning for the whole field of positive psychology. It is one example of what psychologists call metacognition, an umbrella term that means thinking about thinking. Tough (2012) suggests that thinking, talking and evaluating character are all metacognitive processes.

CBT involves using the conscious mind to recognize negative or self-destructive thoughts or interpretations and the skills to talk yourself into a better frame of mind. Tom Brunzell, dean of students at KIPP school in New York city since 2005 believes that the students who succeed at KIPP are the ones who can CBT themselves in the moment. Brunzell sees it part of the job for him and his colleagues to give their students the tools to do that:

> All kids this age are having mini-implosions everyday . . . it's middle school, the worst years of their lives. But the kids who make it are the ones who can tell themselves, 'I can rise above this little situation. I'm okay. Tomorrow is a new day.'
>
> *(quoted in Tough 2012, p. 91)*

Angela Duckworth, however, believes that thinking and talking about character isn't enough. It's one thing to know that that you need to improve your self-control, will power or motivation, but it's another thing to have the tools to do so. Duckworth has devised a variety of strategies, practical psychological techniques based on CBT that enable individuals to build their character strengths. This work, Paul Tough (2012) suggests, is in many ways an extension of her previous work with Walter Mischel.

The famous marshmallow

In the early 1970s, Walter Mischel (then at Stanford University) and his colleagues carried out one of the most famous experiments in modern psychology. The experiment tested the will power of a group of four-year-olds by presenting them with a conflict between a short-term treat and a longer-term reward. Mischel sat a succession of four-year-olds in a room and put a marshmallow on the table (Students at KIPP schools, according to Paul Tough, who visited the school in 2011, wore T-shirts with the slogan 'Don't Eat the Marshmallow' on the back). He told them they could eat the marshmallow straight away but that he was going away and if they waited until he returned they could have two marshmallows. In the videos of the experiment you can see Mischel leave the room and then the children hiding their eyes, banging their heads on the table in an effort to stop themselves eating the marshmallow on the table in front of them.

The notable thing about this experiment is that the four-year-olds who had self control and who could delay gratification and not eat the marshmallow did much better in school, had less behavioural difficulties and better social skills than the children who could only wait a few minutes. Children who could wait a full 15 minutes had, 13 years later, SAT scores that were 210 points higher than the children who could only wait a shorter times. In fact, the marshmallow test turned out to be a better predictor of SAT Scores than the IQ test given to the four-year-olds. Twenty years later the children who could wait longer had much higher college-completion rates and 30 years later had much higher incomes. On the other hand, the children who could not wait at all had much higher rates of imprisonment and were much more likely to suffer from drug and alcohol addiction problems.

The marshmallow test measured whether children had learned strategies to control their impulses. The ones who had control and will power did well in school and life. The ones that didn't do so well found school frustrating and unrewarding. The key finding from the marshmallow experiment concerned the strategies that the children used and that worked for them in terms of enabling them to delay gratification. 'If you knew how to avoid the temptation of a marshmallow as a preschooler, it seemed, you also knew how to get yourself to class on time, finish your homework once you got older, as well as how to make friends and resist peer pressure. It was as if the marshmallow-ignoring children had regulatory skills that subsequently gave them an advantage throughout their lives' (Duhigg 2011, p. 133). The children who did badly in the experiment did not use a strategic approach to avoiding the marshmallow; in fact, they sat and looked straight at it. The children that could wait had techniques to control their attention and used a variety of tactics to distract themselves they pretended the marshmallow wasn't real or that it wasn't even there, they imagined that it had a frame around it and was a picture, or even that it wasn't really a marshmallow; it was a fluffy cloud.

Triggering

The important implication of the marshmallow test is the recognition that self-control is not about will power mastering our passions and overcoming temptations rather its about having the strategies. As Jeremy Dean (2013) explains, the conscious mind simply lacks the strength and awareness to directly control our unconscious processes. Instead its about triggering. Individuals with self-control and self-discipline build habits and strategies that trigger the unconscious processes that allow them to see the world in healthy and far-seeing ways.

Brooks (2011) explains human decision-making has three basic steps. Firstly, we perceive a situation, secondly, we reason whether taking this or that action is in our long-term interest and finally we use power of will to carry out the decision. Although reason and will are important in making decisions, Brooks suggests that the conscious forces of reason and will are in fact not always powerful enough to control our unconscious urges. That's why diets fail, and as Timothy Wilson notes, 'Scared Straight' programmes which aim to deter young people from engaging in unhealthy habits by information programmes alone on the dangers, for example, of smoking, taking drugs or unprotected sex have little direct effect on unconscious impulses. The evidence suggests that reason and will are not very powerful muscles and are too weak to impose self-discipline by themselves.

The most important step in the decision-making process, suggests Brooks (2011), is actually the first one. Perceiving is a thinking and skilful process, and individuals with good character has learnt or have been taught by others to see situations in the correct way and triggered a network of unconscious judgements and responses. Once a situation has been assessed accurately, reason and will then be strong enough to guide proper behaviour. To illustrate this process, Brooks describes how some students will enter a classroom with no innate respect for whatever teacher they may find there. When they get angry or frustrated, they'll swear or ignore the teacher or even become aggressive. Other students, however, walk in to the classroom with innate respect for the teacher and know without thinking about it that there are ways to act in front of a teacher and ways not to act. This does not mean that these students do not get angry or frustrated but rather that they know to express these feelings away from the classroom. It would not occur to such students to vent their anger or frustration openly in the classroom, and if another student did that in their presence, they would be shocked and horrified. Brooks (2011) suggests that innate respect comes from countless influences that may now be unconscious. Maybe these students came to respect the authority of their parents and now extend that respectful attitude to all authority figures. Maybe they have internalised habits and norms about classroom behaviour that automatically inhibits the sorts of behaviour they intuitively know is unacceptable. Similarly, Brooks suggests that decent people learn to see other people's property in a way that rules out the temptation to steal. This model emphasises the power of the community and the power of small and repetitive actions which rewire the neural networks of the brain. Habits reinforce certain positive ways of seeing the world and good behaviour strengthens certain networks. Aristotle was correct when he observed that 'We acquire virtues by first having put them into action'. Timothy Wilson (2011) of the University of Virginia puts it more scientifically when he suggests that one of the most enduring lessons of social psychology is that behaviour change often precedes changes in attitude and feelings.

When a great deal of our behaviour is habitual we need less self-control to make us carry them out and leaves us free for less routine events. Forming positive habits and allowing a healthy structure and routing influence most of our life means that we can retain our reserves of self-control for when it matters. Jennifer Fox Eades (2008, p. 219) suggests that we can exercise our self-control like a muscle. Making a habit of small acts of self-control like politeness, good posture, smart dress can build self-discipline and enable individuals to exercise greater self control in times of stress.

Tough (2012) suggests that in the long run it serves most people well to have conscientiousness as their default position. Because when it does matter – when you have to study for a final exam or show up for a job interview – you will probably make the correct choice and you won't have to exert yourself and exhaust yourself in order to do so.

Mental Contrasting with Implementation Intentions (MCII)

Angela Duckworth has devised what Tough (2012, p. 93) refers to as a 'nuts and bolts' metacognitive strategy because she recognises that:

> just fantasizing about doing your maths homework every day – that feels really good right then – but you don't go out and do anything. When I go into schools, I see posters that say 'Dream it and you can achieve it' but we need to get away from positive fantasizing about how we're all going to grow up to be rich and famous and start thinking about the obstacles that stand in the way and planning effective solutions to getting where we want to be.

The power of rules

MCII was originally developed by New York University psychologist Gabriele Oettingen and her colleagues (see Tough 2012, p. 92). This strategy is about setting *rules* for yourself.

David Kessler explains that the reasons that rules work is because they enlist the prefrontal cortex as your ally against the more reflexive, appetite-driven parts of your brain. Rules are not the same as will power. They are a meta-cognitive substitute for will power. By making yourself a rule, explains Kessler, you are bypassing the painful, internal conflict and your determination to resist a treat. Rules provide structure because they prepare us for encounters with temptations and enable us to redirect our attention elsewhere.

Oettingen discovered that individuals tend to use three strategies when they are setting goals for themselves but only one of these strategies work.

1. Optimists favour 'indulging', which means imagining the future they'd like to achieve and really thinking about all the good things that go along with it: i.e., the praise, the self-satisfaction, and future successes. Oettingen found that although indulging feels good when you are doing it doesn't correlate with actual achievement.
2. Pessimists use 'dwelling', which involves thinking about all the negative things that will get in the way of reaching their goals.
3. The third strategy is called 'contrasting'. Contrasting involves combing elements of both indulging and dwelling. Firstly, it involves imagining a positive vision of the problem solved and at the same time thinking about the obstacles in the way. Oettingen suggests that doing both at the same time

'creates a strong association between future and reality that signals the need to overcome the obstacles in order to attain the goal' (Tough 2012, p. 93).

The next step to a successful outcome is creating the series of 'implementation intentions' – specific plans in the form of if/then that link the obstacles with ways to overcome them. Oettingen has demonstrated the effectiveness of MCII in enabling individuals to build healthy habits such as eating more fruit and vegetables and exercising more, and enabling students to prepare more thoroughly for exams.

Rules

MCII is really about setting rules for yourself. David Kessler suggests that there is a neurobiological reason why rules work.

When you're making rules for yourself, you're using the your prefrontal cortex (i.e., the thinking part of your brain against the more reflexive, appetite-driven parts of your brain). Rules, explains Kessler, are not the same as will power. They are 'a metacognitive' substitute for will power. By making yourself a rule you can avoid the *shall I? / shan't I?* conversation with yourself. 'Rules provide structure, prepare us for encounters with temptation and redirect our attention elsewhere' (Kessler, 2009, pp. 93–94).

Aristotle famously proclaimed 'We are what we repeatedly do, excellence then is not an act but a habit'. Automaticity (i.e., acting without thinking) is a central component of a habit. Studies have suggested that somewhere between one-third and half the time people are engaged in behaviours which are rated as habitual. This suggests that half the time we're awake, we're performing a habit of one kind or another and even this high figure may be an underestimation.

Psychologist Jeremy Dean (2013) describes the three main characteristics of a habit as follows:

1. We are only vaguely aware when we are performing them.
2. The act of performing a habit is emotionless.
3. Our habits are rooted in the situations in which they occur.

Recalling our habits can be a very difficult thing to do because of their 'automaticity', the fact that we engage in them without thinking about what we are doing. Automaticity, however, is also one of the major benefits of a habit because it allows the conscious part of our mind to think about something else while our unconscious gets on with repetitive behaviours. Habits protect us from 'decision fatigue'; they free up our processing power for other thoughts.

The act of performing a habit is emotionless. Like anything in life, as soon as we get used to a habit our emotional responses lessens. Activities which in the beginning can be very painful, for example, getting up very early each morning generally become less so with repetition.

We tend to do the same things in the same circumstances and it's partly this connection between the situation and the behaviour that causes behaviours to form in the first place. Think Ivan Pavlov and his famous research with dogs!

Implicitly we understand habits as the ways in which we act automatically, without needing to think about them. Habits require less effort and resources, both psychological and physical. Understood in this way, it becomes clear how using our character strengths represent a positive, constructive 'good habit'. This is because we are already predisposed and highly motivated to use them, and we feel rewarded when doing so because of the feelings of authenticity and energy that using our strengths generates.

WOOP

Psychologist Jeremy Dean (2013) comments that although MCII is fine in theory, the main problem with mental contrasting is that, in practise, it's hard. Thinking about the negative aspects of a our goals is unpleasant, because suddenly it becomes obvious what we needs to be done and this can be depressing. Also people don't like moving from happy to depressing thoughts. The clash between the fantasy of developing a habit and the obstacles you'll face can be depressing. Jeremy Dean suggests that if you are finding mental contrasting difficult the WOOP exercise can be helpful.

WOOP stands for Wish, Outcome, Obstacle and Plan. First, you write down your wish, the habit you want to achieve, then, the best outcome of your habit, then the obstacles you are likely to face. Finally you make a specific type of plan – an implementation intention plan.

Implementation intention plans

Firstly, we need to break the plan down into two parts, first the *if–then,* which is a trigger for your action. This needs to be specific but not too specific. Dean suggests that instead of saying 'if I reach the lift at work, then I'll use the stairs', a little tweak will make it more realistic. 'If I reach any lift, then I will take the stairs'. It is also important to consider how your habit will fit into your daily routine. Dean suggests avoiding specific times as this can create clock watching and is likely to be unrealistic in the long run. In terms of the *then,* Dean firstly recommends that the simpler the *then* is the easier it will be to carry out, and secondly giving yourself a multiple options, e.g., 'If it's after breakfast and there is time, I will go for a run or ride my bicycle'.

Fixed and growth mindsets

Carol Dweck (2006), who is a professor at Stanford University, has demonstrated that students do much better if they *believe* that intelligence is malleable and can increase. Regardless of whether in fact the purest kind of intelligence is malleable or not, students do much better if they *believe* intelligence *is* malleable. Dweck (2006) and her colleagues identified two different mindsets that students carry around with them: (1) a *fixed* mindset, in which intelligence and other skills are thought of as set in stone; and (2) a *growth* mindset, in which intelligence is seen as dynamic and capable of improvement. Dweck set out to investigate how these different mindsets affect performance.

Scott Barry Kaufman (2013) assistant professor of psychology at New York University writes that even the most well-intentioned teachers can send damaging messages to their students. Dweck found that that praising the ability of students after doing well on a test promoted a fixed view of ability, whereas praising the effort that contributed to the performance led to a growth mindset. Kaufman emphasises that this difference matters. Those who are praised for their ability showed a drop in intrinsic motivation, confidence and performance when they later encountered difficult problems whereas those praised for their effort maintained their levels of motivation and performance when they faced future challenges.

In a recent study (cited in Kaufman 2013) found that teachers who held a fixed theory of intelligence were significantly more likely to diagnose a student as having low ability based upon a single, initially poor, performance. They were also more likely to 'comfort' the student for their low ability, saying things like 'It's OK – not everyone can be good at math', which in fact did reduce student's engagement with school subjects. Also, students who were exposed to comfort-orientated messages reported less motivation, expected lower grades, and viewed their teachers as having lower engagement in their learning. The researchers noted that 'the popular practise today of identifying weaknesses and turning students towards their strengths may be another self-esteem-building strategy gone awry, and one that may contribute to the low numbers of students pursuing math and science' (p. 118).

Tough (2012) suggests that Dweck's notion that students do better when they think they can improve their intelligence applies to character as well. Thus the importance of presenting character traits to students not as fixed traits but as a series of constantly developing attributes will inspire them to improve those traits. Tough (2012, p. 98) quotes Mike Witter, an English teacher at a KIPP school who he considers to be hard-wired to believe in the growth mindset: 'If you're going to be a good teacher, you *have* to be believe in malleable intelligence and character is equally malleable. If you teach kids to pay attention to character their character will transform.'

Factors that contribute to an individual's resilience combine exponentially

Building up a young person's character strengths is a vital part of ensuring that an individual is resilient. A well-resourced individual has more strengths to call on to help them when the going gets tough. Positive psychologist Michael Ungar (2006) explains that strengths or resources don't just build one on top of the other. The more there are the greater the effect. Having one characteristic that bolsters resilience is good. Two is even better but the real difference comes when we start having three. Three resources are experienced as if we have four. If we have four characteristics or resources that make us resilient, it is the equivalent of having eight good things to say about ourselves.

A SMART investment

John Yeager et al. (2011) cautions however that there are no simple 'just add water' programs for building a strengths approach. Success is a combination of teachers and students both understanding and using their respective strengths to develop trust and enhance classroom partnerships. By developing a common strengths language in the classroom, teachers and students can create an environment which is characterised by increased achievement and flourishing. John Yeager suggests that making Positive Education a reality can be achieved by practitioners making what he calls a SMART investment.

A SMART investment

> Spotting: When you know your own strengths, you are a better observer of strengths in others and are more attentive to spotting what is good instead of trying to find fault.
>
> Managing: Your family of strengths can be promoted for bringing out the best in you and others. In the classroom this improves student engagement and achievement.
>
> Advocating: Learning to advocate with your strengths will help you build a bridge from yourself to others. When you put your learning into your own words and actions, you can effectively convey both your strengths and your needs.
>
> Relating: Good pupil-teacher and pupil-pupil relationships are about using strengths while connecting and appealing to others.
>
> Training: Once you have tools you will want to use them to develop these skills in your students (Yeager, Fisher, and Shearon 2011, p. 65).

A word of warning

A strengths approach should not be confused with ignoring problems and difficulties, rather it is about focusing on what is going well. Working from a strengths perspective is far more motivating for both students and practitioners than addressing weakness and deficits.

Interventions can have lasting effects

Wilson (2011) suggests that strengths-based interventions can have lasting effects. It is extremely motivating for young people to have their strengths identified and acknowledged and better still the behaviour can become self-sustaining. Individuals adopt a new behaviour or habit that in turn triggers a revision of their self-views; 'I must be the sort of person who really cares about others'. The key to this approach is that individuals develop a more positive view of themselves that build on and reinforces itself leading to sustained change.

Positive Education

Thanks to an abundant body of research by positive psychologists, we now know for sure that there is not a contradiction between happiness and achievement and that both are fully embodied in Seligman's (2011) concept of Positive Education. Autonomy support is the process of giving students a sense of inner independence and thus encouraging their resilience and self-reliance. For the purpose of the programmes that are introduced in the later sections of this book the distinction between making and encouraging is vital. We can encourage but we cannot make others flourish.

The programmes aim to enable students to understand that happiness and well-being for all of us is at least in part about how we think about ourselves and our place in the world. It's not about things. Key messages include that helps to be optimistic and to view ourselves as strong individuals with a sense of purpose, that happiness is at least partly in our heads and some ways of viewing the world make us happier, even if our objective circumstances remain the same.

Note

1   N.B. Not all positive psychologists working with strengths are doing so from a 'values' perspective. The Clifton Strengths Finder (Clifton and Anderson 2002), for example, consists of a longer list that are more focused on business skills.

   At www.cappeu.com (the Centre for Applied Positive Psychology), you can take a comprehensive test for a small fee. This assessment tool allows you to hold many top strengths, as well as highlighting the strengths you don't use enough and those strengths that you could pay more attention to.

   The Realise2 online strengths assessment tool of 60 strengths, from Action to Work Ethic tells you about your own strengths, learned behaviours and weaknesses. It is available at www.strengths2020.com

Section 2
PowerPoint presentation

This section contains notes to support the facilitator in delivering a PowerPoint presentation of 20 slides. The purpose of the presentation is to introduce staff to the main principles of positive psychology and how they can be employed in the classroom to enhance student achievement.

In preparation for the session participants should take 20 minutes to find their VIA (Values in Action) character strengths at www.authentichappiness. com (VIA signature strengths questionnaire).

Slide 1 Using positive psychology to enhance student achievement: using the hidden power of character

Facilitator notes
The aim of this presentation is threefold.

First, it will introduce staff to the main principles of positive psychology and introduce its connection with a 'strengths approach' and character development.

Second, it will provide practitioners with how these concepts impact and influence student achievement.

Third, it will provide practitioners with a guide to delivering the programmes.

Slide 2 What is positive psychology?

Positive psychology is an umbrella term for the scientific study of optimal human functioning: what makes people happier, more productive and more successful. Backed up by scientific rigour, positive psychology provides us with scientific evidence of the qualities and skills that contribute to a fulfilling, healthy and flourishing life.

Positive psychology is not meant to replace traditional psychology and what is known about human suffering, weakness and disorder. The aim is to have a complete and balanced understanding of the human experience.

Facilitator notes
The positive psychology movement began in 1998 when Martin Seligman, who is generally acknowledged as the architect of this relatively new science, was inaugurated as President of the American Psychological Society. Its main purpose is to redress the traditional tilt of psychology that focused on human weakness.

Positive psychology is about rebalancing our interests to highlight the fact that happiness is not simply the opposite of unhappiness. Most of psychological studies that have been carried out over the past 40 years have focused on the negative side of life such as anxiety, depression, low self-esteem and post-traumatic stress disorder. Positive psychologists set out to redress this balance by focusing on the human qualities and circumstances which lead to flourishing and by demonstrating that strengths have their own patterns, i.e., they are not simply the opposite of weaknesses and disorders and therefore need to be studied in their own right.

Research within this field has grown considerably over the last few years, and there is now the data to prove the substantial control that people have over their happiness and well-being.

Activity

Provide an opportunity for participants to ask questions and/or seek clarification on positive psychology.

Ask participants to discuss in pairs what they understand by the terms happiness, well-being and flourishing.

Ask for feedback.

Slide 3 'Subjective well-being' is the technical term for happiness

Well-being has five measurable elements (PERMA):

1. **P**ositive emotions of which happiness and life satisfaction are key elements
2. **E**ngagement
3. **R**elationships
4. **M**eaning
5. **A**chievement

(Seligman 2011)

Facilitator notes

Although the terms well-being, happiness and flourishing have similar meanings in the positive psychology literature, there are some recognised differences in what these terms convey. Martin Seligman has recently announced that his thinking has moved on and that he now 'detests the term happiness, which is now so overused that it has become almost meaningless' (Seligman, 2011, p. 24). He suggests that it is an unworkable term because the modern ear immediately hears 'happy' to mean smiley faces, good mood, pleasure and fun.

There are, of course those who would disagree with Seligman's criticism of the term 'happiness' and continue to associate the term with the classical teachings of Aristotle. Aristotle rejected the idea that happiness meant pleasure and believed that it stood for 'eudaimonia', i.e., leading a virtuous life.

Seligman now considers that the main topic of positive psychology to be well-being. Happiness is only one component of well-being. The gold standard for measuring well-being is in terms of flourishing.

One of the valuable outcomes of the popularity of positive psychology is that we now have a larger vocabulary for describing the positive aspects of life.

Activity
Provide an opportunity for participants to ask questions and seek clarification on the terms 'happiness', 'well-being' and 'flourishing'.

Slide 4 Flourishing

To flourish an individual needs the three core features of well-being:

1. Positive emotion (or happiness)
2. Engagement and interest
3. Meaning and purpose

and three of the six additional features:

1. self-esteem
2. optimism
3. resilience
4. vitality
5. self-determination
6. positive relationships

(Huppert and So, quoted in Seligman 2011)

Facilitator notes
Based on Seligman's rethink of positive psychology:

- well-being has taken centre stage
- happiness is now only part of the bigger picture of well-being
- flourishing is the outcome of well-being

Activity
Ask participants to think about a student they currently work with and consider the features of flourishing this young person demonstrates.

   Take feedback.

Slide 5 The power of positive emotions

Barbara Frederikson's (2001) Broaden and Build Theory of Positive Emotions is one of the cornerstones of positive psychology. She discovered that in contrast to negative emotions, which have the effect of narrowing our focus, thoughts and behaviours to specific, self-protecting behaviours, positive emotions encourage creative, exploratory thoughts and behaviours.

Over time, this broadened behavioural repertoire builds additional personal resources and skills in four main categories:

1. Intellectual, e.g., developing our problem-solving skills
2. Physical, e.g., developing our physical strength
3. Social, e.g., improving the quality and quantity of our friendships and other relationships and connections
4. Psychological, e.g., developing our resilience and optimism.

Facilitator notes

Barbara Frederikson's goal in carrying out this research was to find out if positive emotions have a purpose apart from making us feel good.

She discovered that positive emotions don't just feel good, they do us good too.

Negative emotions, such as fear and anger, lead to narrow, self-protecting actions; for example, anger leads to a desire to fight, and fear leads to a desire to run.

The experience of positive emotions, on the other hand, opens our minds and creates 'upward' spirals of thought and action and increased social ties and expanded skills. These enable us to take on future challenges and seek out and work towards new goals.

Activity

When we feel positive, we are better able to react and respond positively to our environment, which in turn builds more resources. Have participants pair up, and then ask them to discuss their experiences in the work place of how positive emotions have expanded their feelings of confidence and enabled them to take on new challenges.

Take feedback.

Slide 6 Flow

According to Seligman, 'engagement' is an essential component of well-being. Engagement is achieved through flow.

Coined by the Russian psychologist Mihaly Csikszentmihalyi (pronounced 'cheeks-sent-me-high-ee'), *flow* is a term that describes a state of optimal experience.

Experiencing flow is beneficial because it produces positive emotions, leads to personal growth, encourages persistence with challenging tasks, and leads to the development of skills.

Flow is linked to academic commitment and achievement, better physical health and improved self-esteem.

The balance of challenge to skill is essential in creating a flow experience:

- High challenge + medium to high skill = flow
- High challenge + low skill = anxiety and stress
- Low challenge + medium to high skill = apathy and boredom

Facilitator notes

According to Dr Mihaly Csikszentmihalyi, the world is chaotic. Finding and constructing order and being engaged with the world is an essential aspect of flow.

A state of flow can be achieved if your skills match your competencies, there are clear goals, and you know how you are progressing towards them.

Being in a state of flow can enable us to grow and flourish.

Activity

Ask participants to spend a few minutes identifying those activities which enable them to achieve flow, i.e., the times they find themselves so immersed and absorbed in an activity that time flies unnoticed.

Jenny Fox Eades (2008, p. 28) writes that in her experience children, especially younger children do not achieve flow in school as often as we might wish. With a partner, discuss what a flow-friendly classroom would look like.

Take feedback.

Slide 7 Growth and fixed mindset

Neuroscientists have discovered the 'neuro-plasticity' of the human brain, i.e., its capacity to grow and develop into old age. Carol Dweck (2006) has introduced the concept of 'cognitive fitness', the ability to improve our brain and intelligence through developing a 'growth mindset'.

- If you have a **growth mindset,** you believe that your intelligence, personal qualities and abilities can grow and develop over time.
- If you have a **fixed mindset,** you believe that your intelligence, personal qualities and abilities are carved in stone and cannot grow.

Our mindsets can have a significant impact upon our behaviour, the goals we set ourselves and how we respond to setbacks and failure.

Facilitator notes

Carol Dweck's research suggests that individuals with a fixed mindset get depressed, lose self-confidence and tend to give up if they fail to reach their goal. According to Dweck, those with a fixed mindset are likely to say 'I'll never be able to do it so I won't try again'.

For growth-mindset individuals, failure isn't such a big deal. Rather than focusing on how they feel, they focus on what they can learn from the experience, which helps them to do better next time and they're more willing to try new approaches in order to improve. Doing badly in an exam doesn't mean they're stupid; it's simply a reflection of how they are doing at this particular moment in time and focus on what they can learn from the experience that will improve their performance next time.

Activity

Studies suggest that fixed-mindset individuals typically say that intelligence is 35 per cent effort and 65 per cent ability. Growth-mindset individuals, on the other hand, say that its 65 per cent effort and 35 per cent ability.

With a partner discuss what you think about intelligence.

How much is intelligence about the effort you make and how much is about your ability?

Slide 8 Wishing others well: WOW

One of the core principles of positive psychology is that 'other people matter'.

Positive relationships with others, our engagement both with individuals and with the community are central to our well-being and enable us to flourish.

The concept of an emotional bank account was devised by Stephen Covey (1999). It emphasises the idea that relationships are something that we should invest in. We can make deposits (actions we take to build our relationships) and also make withdrawals (actions we take to neglect or even harm our relationships).

Facilitator notes

Seligman (2011) repeatedly emphasises the importance of our relationships with a variety of others to enable us to flourish. The foremost study on the very happiest people revealed the quality that all these individuals share is the existence of strong, supportive relationships in their lives. Chris Peterson, one of the leaders in positive psychology, has been know to say that there is no such thing as a happy hermit.

Activity

Ask participants to discuss the concept of an emotional bank account and suggest what sort of positive habits and ways of relating to students and colleagues could be introduced in the school/setting in order to enhance relationships.

Take feedback.

Slide 9 Active gratitude

Seligman et al. (2005) have suggested that having a habit of writing down three good things that went well for you and giving an explanation for why they happened to you can make you measurably happier.

It's as if the habit of counting your blessings and understanding why they happened makes them multiply.

Emmons (2007) calls this process 'active gratitude' and describes it as a felt sense of wonder, thankfulness and appreciation for life.

Essentially this exercise works by re-educating our attention to identify what is good in life.

Facilitator notes

Active gratitude involves a focus on the present moment and on the things we have rather than what we do not have. Emmons suggests that practising the habit of active gratitude can make us happier and more energetic and enable us to experience more frequent, positive feelings. Also, if we practise the habit of active gratitude, we are less likely to be depressed, anxious, lonely or depressed.

Activity

Ask participants to take a few moments to practise the Three Good Things exercise, i.e., write down three good things that have happened to them and why. Remind participants to focus their attention specifically on the here and now.

Slide 10 Mindfulness

Mindfulness has been defined as paying attention in a particular way:

- on purpose
- in the present moment
- non-judgementally

It's about being able to tune into what's happening in and around us in a conscious and purposeful way.

Five essential steps to mindfulness:

1. be non-judgemental
2. accept things as they are
3. notice thoughts and emotions as they occur
4. be fully in the moment
5. be observant

(Grenville-Cleave 2012)

Facilitator notes

Mindfulness is a specific type of meditation-based practise which has been gaining in popularity in the Western world over the past 30 years or so.

Encouraging students to get into a routine of practising mindfulness as a technique for increasing focus and reducing stress is associated with a number of benefits. These include:

- better control of emotions
- decreased dwelling on negative thoughts
- reduced depression and anxiety
- decreased emotional reactivity
- more flexible thinking

- increased positive emotion
- decreased negative emotion

Activity

Mindful breathing is a simple technique which is at the heart of mindfulness.
   You can begin to practise mindfulness anywhere; have a go now.
   Spend a few moments practising mindful breathing.

Slide 11 Signature character strengths

Chris Peterson and Martin Seligman (2004) identified 24 signature (higher) character strengths. They are organised into the six virtues which are universal characteristics:

1. Wisdom and knowledge
2. Courage
3. Love and humanity
4. Justice
5. Temperance
6. Transcendence

   Building strengths and virtues is about discovery, creation and ownership.
   'Positive emotion leads to exploration which leads to mastery and mastery leads not only to more positive emotion but also to an individual's signature strengths' (Seligman 2003).
   Being able to put a name to what one does well is intriguing and empowering.

Facilitator notes

Distribute copies of the hand-out to participants. This is reproduced on pp. 13–14.
   According to Seligman and Peterson, the value of these 24 character strengths does not come from their relationship to any particular system of ethics but from their practical benefit – what we can gain by possessing and expressing them. Cultivating these strengths represents a reliable path to 'the good life', a life that is not just happy but also meaningful and fulfilling.
   Character can often refer to something that is innate and unchanging, a set of attributes that define who one is. Seligman and Peterson defined character in a different way: a set of abilities or strengths that are very much changeable. They are skills that you can learn, practise and teach.

Activity

Ask participants to read the hand-out 'Values in Action, Classification of Character Strengths' and consider how this list relates to:

- building positive relationships with others
- engaging in purposeful activity
- finding meaning in our lives

   Ask for feedback.

Slide 12 Character strengths are simple habits

William James, the American philosopher and psychologist, believed that the traits we call virtues or character strengths are no more or less than simple habits.

James believed that it is the responsibility of education to chaperone the formation of habit:

> First, we must make automatic and habitual as early as possible, as many useful actions as we can and guard against the growing into ways that are likely to be disadvantageous to us, as we should guard against the plague. The more details of our daily life that we can hand over to the effortless custody of automatism, the more our higher powers of mind will be set free for their own proper work. There is no more miserable human being than one in whom nothing is habitual but indecision.
>
> *(William James, Habit, public library, public domain)*

Facilitator notes

In the tradition of Aristotle and William James, Martin Seligman and his colleague Angela Duckworth have explored ways to ensure that students understand the importance of and develop good habits. This means that they have made it their default position to do the 'good' thing meaning the more socially acceptable or chosen the long-term–benefit enhancing option. Duckworth (quoted in Seligman 2011) says, 'It's not like some kids are good and some kids are bad. Some kids have good habits and some kids have bad habits. Kids understand it when you put it that way, because they know that habits might be *hard* to change but they are not *impossible* to change. William James says our nervous systems are like a sheet of paper. You fold it over and over again and pretty soon you have a crease. . . . you want to make sure that they have the sorts of creases that will lead them to success later on'.

Activity

Provide an opportunity for participants to discuss the idea that character strengths are in fact habits.

Slide 13 Excellence as a habit

Aristotle famously proclaimed: 'We are what we repeatedly do, excellence then is not an act but a habit.'

Facilitator notes

'Automaticity', which means acting without thinking, is a central component of a habit. Studies have suggested that somewhere between one-third and half the time people are engaged in behaviours which are rated as habitual. This suggests that half the time we're awake, we're performing a habit of one kind or another and even this high figure may be underestimated.

Activity

Ask participants to consider the sorts of habits that make up our daily lives.

Slide 14 The three main characteristics of a habit

1. We are only vaguely aware when we are performing them.
2. The act of performing a habit is emotionless.
3. Our habits are rooted in the situations in which they occur.

(Dean 2013)

Facilitator notes

Recalling our habits can be a very difficult thing to do because of their 'automaticity', the fact that we engage in habits without thinking about what we are doing. One of the major benefits of a habit is that it allows the conscious part of our mind think about something else while our unconscious gets on with repetitive behaviours. Habits protect us from 'decision fatigue'; they free up our processing power for other thoughts.

The act of performing a habit is emotionless. Like anything in life, as soon as we get used to a habit our emotional responses lessens. Activities which in the beginning can be very painful, like getting up very early, become less so with repetition.

We tend to do the same things in the same circumstances and its partly this connection between the situation and the behaviour that causes behaviours to form in the first place. Think Ivan Pavlov and his famous research with dogs!

Activity

Provide participants with an opportunity to discuss what these three characteristics of a habit mean for their work. What can be done in schools and settings to enable children and young people to build healthy habits?

Slide 15 SLANT

Facilitator notes

David Levin and Michael Feinberg, co-founders of the Knowledge is Power Programme (KIPP) charter schools in America, had long been concerned about the dropout rate at university of students from the poorest backgrounds at the KIPP schools. They realized that those who were succeeding at university were not necessarily those who had been the top students at KIPP but were those who possessed character strengths, particularly resilience and tenacity. Levin and Feinberg worked with Martin Seligman and subsequently made several of Peterson and Seligman's Character Strengths as the cornerstones of their schools. They chose self-control, grit, social intelligence, optimism, gratitude and curiosity as the basis of their character education programme.

One of the very practical steps they took was to introduce in all their schools SLANT, a very practical set of classroom habits that enable students to code-switch and recognise and accurately perform every time without fail the professional behaviours appropriate to the classroom as opposed to the street.

SLANT stands for Sit up, Listen, Ask questions, Nod and Track the speaker with your eyes.

Activity
Provide an opportunity for participants to:

- Identify some of the classroom habits which are already established in their school/setting.
- Brainstorm practical suggestions for further developing this work.

Take feedback.

Slide 16 Building positive habits

Positive psychology can help us to build positive habits of thought, speech and behaviour. Firstly, in ourselves, and then in the students we work with.

Each thought we have creates a neural pathway in our brain. Constantly think negative thoughts and you reinforce those mental pathways and make it more likely that your next thought will be gloomy.

Each positive thought we have creates a positive mental pathway and strengthens our capacity to think positively, to notice what is good (Fox Eades 2008).

Facilitator notes
Martin Seligman (2011) has recently coined the term 'positive education'. Positive education means using the findings of positive psychology studies in our day-to-day work in schools.

Activity
Ask participants to review the studies that were introduced earlier in this presentation and consider how the findings can be used to create positive habits of thought, speech and behaviour in the workplace.

Take feedback.

Slide 17 Introduction to the programme

The programme, which consists of a resource bank of activities, has been designed in order to introduce students to the key insights of positive psychology.

The activities aim to teach students the skills that are essential for building optimism and resilience, how to recognise and combat negative thoughts that bring about loss of self-esteem and even depression and to understand that there are certain ways of thinking that they can use to make their lives go better.

The resources emphasise a character-strength approach. Studies now suggest that in terms of achievement, character is as important as IQ.

Activity

Provide an opportunity for participants to ask questions about the content and delivery of the programme.

Slide 18 The resources are in three parts

The resources are presented in three parts:

- Building Habits
- Happy Habits
- Friendly Habits

Facilitator notes

The activities in Part 1, Building habits, introduce the concept of a habit and take the students through the process of defining a habit, what constitutes happiness and the types of habits that reinforce well-being. Part 1 consists of 33 activities.

The activities in Part 2 focus on Happy Habits and introduce a wide range of key skills and strategies for students to use to promote their well-being.

There is an emphasis on managing and controlling feelings and guidance for developing strategies to build confidence, manage stress, visualisation and savouring.

Part 2 consists of 49 activities.

The activities in Part 3 focus on Friendly Habits. These are the sorts of habits which aim to develop the skills of empathy, being a good friend, alongside the ability to maintain a positive outlook. Part 3 consists of 33 activities.

Activity

Provide an opportunity for participants to ask questions about the content and delivery of the programme.

Slide 19 Practical activity

Activity

Distribute a selection of copies of the activities from each of the three parts of the programme and ask participants to work with a partner and suggest ways that they would use the activity.

Take feedback

Slide 20 Peak end rule

Optimism, flow and happy memories are essential to happiness.

(Seligman 2003)

Emotional memories depend on how an experience concludes.

(Frederickson 2001)

Facilitator notes

Celebrating is a provocative act. It is about focusing on what is good in life, what has gone well and building shared and happy memories.

Positive psychology teaches us that we get more of what we focus on so if we celebrate regularly we will find even more to celebrate. Celebration builds relationships and makes good things happen. It improves our mood and enables us to feel positive about ourselves and others.

Positive psychologists put a particular emphasis on positive endings because studies suggest that our emotional memories depend on how an experience ends. Thus practitioners invariably ensure that lessons and the school day end on a positive note. Children's parties usually conclude with a goody bag.

It is important to conclude activities and events with a focus on positive moments and what has gone well, Consciously ending on a high note is called `peak end rule' and is what will help to make any difficulties disappear when we look back and reflect on the event.

Activity

Celebrating is a habit that can significantly increase our well-being. Ask participants to explore with a partner how they can build the habit of celebrating into their work.

Conclude the session by asking participants to share with a partner what went well for them during the session.

Take feedback.

Thank participants for attending the session and wish them success in delivering the programme.

Section 3
How to use these resources

Introduction

The resources introduce students to the key insights of positive psychology; i.e., the importance of being connected to others, making and keeping friends, using and celebrating strengths and holding a thoughtful attitude rather than being reactive to whatever happens to us. The activities aim to teach students the skills that are essential for building optimism and resilience, how to recognise and combat negative thoughts that bring about loss of self-esteem and even depression and to understand that there are certain ways of thinking that they can employ to make their lives go better.

Virtues and flourishing

Seligman's recent work emphasises that in order for children and young people to flourish practitioners need to explicitly and systematically ensure that 'virtues', i.e., character strengths, become an inextricable part of the learning process. This is why, when working through this resource bank, students are asked to identify their own character strengths and consider how they can further develop and use these in their daily lives. Character strengths enable us to persist, or 'keep at it', when we feel like giving up. This is why they are also central to this resource. Flourishing means getting on with things that are important for an individual to do, exercising one's talents, actively working to 'realise' what you care about and bring it to life. Being 'in the flow' and experiencing the joy of creativity and meaningful activity is also actively encouraged throughout this resource.

Seligman (2011) argues that the qualities that matter most are to do with character: skills like perseverance, curiosity, conscientiousness, optimism and self-control, and he has therefore introduced the term 'positive education' to indicate that character is an integral part of achievement and flourishing.

This resource bank is unique because it emphasises a character-strength approach; in other words, in terms of achievement, character is as, if not more important than talent. Positive psychologists argue that 'even if children have the academic skills they need, if they don't also have strong character skills then they don't have very much' (Tough, 2012). Character is what keeps people happy, successful and fulfilled. Ultimately, this is the core aim of this resource – to help children and young people to develop, build and practise a range of 'Happy Habits'.

Character training

Character training is a metacognitive strategy. The children who succeed are the ones that can do cognitive behaviour therapy on themselves and who in times of difficulty can say to themselves 'I can rise above this situation. I'm fine. Tomorrow is a new day'. This is why many of the activities in this resource bank make use of tools and strategies from both cognitive behaviour therapy and mindfulness approaches. Seligman (2011) suggests that the most fruitful time to transform children so that they are 'metacognitive' (capable of thinking about thinking) is in late childhood and before puberty. Talking about character, thinking about character and evaluating character are all metacognitive processes. Paul Tough (2012) suggests, however, that thinking and talking is not enough. It's one thing to know that you have to improve your perseverance, for example, but it's another to actually have the tools to do so. Just as a strong will doesn't help much if a student isn't motivated to succeed, so motivation isn't enough without the willpower to follow through on goals.

Developing rules and happy habits

What children need to do in order to be successful is to be motivated and to have willpower; in practical terms this means that they need to be able to set themselves rules and stick to them. There is a neurobiological reason why rules work. When you are making rules for yourself, you're enlisting the pre-frontal cortex as your partner against the more reflexive, appetite-driven parts of your brain. Rules are not, however, the same as will power. Psychologists have shown that by making yourself a rule you are side-stepping the internal conflict between your desire for a treat, for example, and your wilful determination to resist it. Rules provide structure, preparing us for encounters with temptations and successfully redirecting our attention elsewhere. Over time rules become automatic. This, in effect, is the rationale for presenting 'rules' as 'happy habits' – if we can train ourselves to stick to a series of happiness rules or habits on a daily basis, then we are more likely to further maintain and develop overall well-being, remaining optimistic and resilient and more able to cope with the challenges we face, and not give up or become overly stressed in times of trouble. We ultimately want the happiness habit to become automatic!

Using the resource bank across the curriculum/school context

This scheme of work consequently provides a comprehensive programme for supporting the development of young people's social and emotional skills within a safe and positive context and framework. The development and roll-out of the social and emotional aspects of learning (SEAL) curriculum and approaches department for education and skills (DFES) and an increase in the overall awareness of the importance of developing these skills of emotional literacy has been raised significantly in recent years. It now appears to be more commonly accepted that basic social skills and the development of an emotional vocabulary are essential prerequisites. Young people need these skills if they are to develop appropriately and function effectively within both the social and learning contexts. The development of such skills is also much more likely to ensure academic success, and this 'emotional intelligence' is probably the most powerful predictor of future life success (Goleman 2007). Given that there had been such a relevant and recent focus upon the development of these skills alongside opportunities for staff training across all key stages, it can safely be assumed that the majority of school-based staff will have some idea regarding the need to foster well-being within such an emotionally literate context.

Building happy habits and making use of key tools and strategies from positive psychology can be seen as a direct result of the work in this area over the last 10 years. Many schools will have made use of a range of programmes, including SEAL, in order to promote such awareness and the development of life skills and well-being in general. As with this programme, these can be delivered in personal social and health education (PSHE) lessons, assemblies or in every curriculum area. For example, the school team may well see the value and the evidence base for adopting mindfulness approaches at key moments of the school day or in devising opportunities for children and young people to use their CBT knowledge and skills base as part of a peer mentoring/counselling process. The opportunities are endless for the creative practitioner who is committed to ensuring the well-being and mental health of the children and young people in his/her care. Happy habits can and should permeate every lesson and approach to teaching and learning. If this does happen, then we are convinced that standards of both achievement and behaviour will also rise but most importantly, so will the mental health of the children and young people in our care.

The importance of evaluation systems

While it would seem a given that school staff and their students all benefit from such programmes (in conjunction with the embedding of SEAL across the whole school curriculum and policy-making process), it is also important to ensure appropriate identification and evaluation systems are in place. When a whole school initiative of this kind is undertaken then evaluation is paramount – particularly in identifying improvements (or otherwise) in pupils' behaviour and attitudes to learning. There are also a number of standardised and non-standardised measures available to staff which enable them to assess students' levels of emotional literacy and well-being, e.g., PASS (Pupil Attitude to Self & School) and Emotional Literacy Assessment & Intervention (Southampton Psychology Service). These provide an initial screening in order to highlight students most at risk and provide an evidence-based means of designing the most appropriate interventions. They also enable teachers to assess whether particular sections of the school community are feeling marginalised, ignored, demotivated or at risk of emotional vulnerability affecting their learning. The former tool also allows for pre- and post-intervention measures, i.e., how well did the student respond? How successful was the intervention in terms of changing negative self-perceptions, attitudes and behaviours and in building happy habits?

It is also important to continually recognise the fact that secondary school students experience an enormous range in terms of subject areas, teachers and teaching styles. Any assessment process used to identify either academic or emotional development will need to take account of the ways in which they think, feel and act, in a range of different contexts. It is consequently essential for all staff involved to provide their views as to the behaviours and emotional responses of individual students. Another useful assessment tool fit for such a purpose is the Behaviour Survey Checklist (Jolly and McNamara 1991) and a computerised adaptation of this (Pupil Behaviour Assessment System; PBAS). They are both useful tools in terms of assessing how students' behaviours and attitudes are influenced by context and also for revealing any particular skills and competencies that may present as problematic across a range of classroom contexts. However, the Emotional Literacy Assessment & Intervention package also provides for input from staff, pupil and parent/carers in terms of assessing these skills (via checklists) whilst also subsequently advising on strategies for promoting the key skills within the student and making appropriate environmental changes. We would strongly recommend that staff consider such tools in terms of providing pre- and post-measures of interventions such as this one which emanates from the school of positive psychology and the range of therapeutic interventions for which we know there is now a growing evidence base.

The resources

The resources are presented in three parts, all of which aim to build happy habits and use the hidden power of character. The activity and information sheets are easy to use and transparent in terms of both content and instructions. We have designed the resource so that the facilitator can work through the activities during PSHE or form time on a regular basis over a three-term period. Alternatively, the resources can be used by children and young people in a smaller group or one-to-one sessions as deemed appropriate. The idea here is to be flexible and focus upon key areas for students or groups as and when needed. We did not want to just create a 'fixed' programme or number of sessions which might then constrain the facilitator but rather a set of resources which can be used in a variety of ways and contexts and really begin to support the development of happier habits and ways of thinking, feeling and behaving. Key to this is the need to really familiarise yourself with the contents and to then identify those which will be most appropriate for the individual, small group or whole class of students who will be working on their skills and well-being. This is therefore the rational for presenting the resources initially in three sections. However, the next part of the resource does present a 10-part structured programme for those who would feel more comfortable of find it more appropriate to work in this way and follow a more structured intervention.

Part 1 Building habits

These activities focus on building habits and introduces the concept of a habit and the need to develop 'happy habits'. This is probably why it may be helpful to begin with this part; however, you may wish to deliver the resource in either part or whole as stated earlier, so once again, the need for the facilitator to use some initiative and reflect upon the needs of individuals and groups will be paramount.

The activity and information sheets take the students through the process of defining a habit and what constitutes happiness and the kinds of habits that reinforce well-being and a positive outlook. There is also a focus upon building the self-acceptance habit, and boosting of positive emotions through developing realistic goals and the use of positive thinking and mindfulness strategies and techniques.

The resources are arranged as follows:

1. What is a habit? Distinguishing between good and bad habits in our lives begins the process of highlighting what we should be doing in terms of developing the kinds of habits which promote and further develop well-being.
2. What is happiness? Focusing on what it means to feel good and to be 'flourishing'.
3. A happiness information sheet to reinforce key concepts and ideas.
4. My happiness – a self-reflection activity to prompt deeper thinking into personal experience.
5. Ten habits to happier living – things we can do to live happier lives.
6. Happiness log format which can be used to reflect upon behaviours and responses over time.
7. Acceptance cards – an activity to prompt us to accept and value ourselves as unique human beings.
8. My happiness shield – a visualisation strategy to counteract negativity and protect ourselves via positive affirmations.
9. Identifying positive traits and focusing on the importance of maintaining such a habit.
10. The best habit – self-acceptance checklist which can be used to reinforce the importance of accepting ourselves for who and what we are whilst also thinking about how we can further build upon our strengths.
11. A happy school? – This is a questionnaire for students to assess the happiness factors in their own school context and to think how this can be further increase over time.
12. Self-reflection questions – building the habit of reflecting upon things that we do well, good times and positive personal characteristics.

13. The mindfulness habit – Introduction to mindfulness and how this approach to meditation can support overall well-being which is then followed by a series of mindful activities which can be practised on a regular basis.
14. A mindful breathing activity to practise.
15. A mindful observation activity to practise.
16. More mindful breathing to work on.
17. The raisin exercise.
18. A mindful visualisation.
19. A mindful relaxation activity.
20. The happiness ratio which introduces the 3:1 ratio and asks the students to balance negative and positive words and phrases.
21. Boosting positive emotions which describes three ways of managing emotions via active, calming and thinking techniques.
22. Boosting positive emotions using a positive remembering strategy which helps to recall and reinforce the 'good' times and their associated feelings.
23. My positive scroll is an activity which again reinforces the positives and provides an opportunity to articulate all the good things that have happened over a weekly period.
24. Developing grit is a key concept in that a major route to happiness and well-being is the skill and habit of being able to persevere even when things get tough – not giving up at the first (or second or third) sign of failure or setback. This is a self-reflection quiz which highlights the measure of perseverance and effort of the individual and questions what he or she can do in order to persevere when the going gets tough.
25. Self-reflection activity which focuses on the future and helps to articulate actions which can in turn ensure that dreams and ambitions become a reality in the future.
26. Setting my goals – a good habit. This activity helps the student to articulate a priority goal.
27. Climb the mountain activity enables the student to distinguish between the easiest and most difficult goals to achieve and presents a self-help strategy for use on a regular basis.
28. Change your behaviour helps to identify the things that the student would like to do more often.
29. Take up the challenge helps to identifying more detailed steps to success and utilises coping self-talk and visualisation strategies.
30. Money facts is an activity which encourages reflection around the ways in which money may or may not make us happier and healthier and supports reflection on this topic.
31. What impacts on our happiness is another thinking and self-reflection activity.
32. Five happy habits helps support the identification of a target and a personal strategy for each habit.
33. Get the flow habit introduces the concept of flow and supports the identification of activities which enable us to experience this sense of flow and also highlights how important such experience is for our overall well-being on a daily basis.

Part 2 Happy habits

These activities focus specifically on happy habits and introduce a wide range of key skills and strategies for the children and young people to practise and use. There are opportunities to further understand the need to manage and control feelings that may be unhelpful, and to develop strategies to specifically manage such feelings such as relaxation. There is also a focus on identifying, developing and using skills and strengths to do this. Building confidence, managing stress, visualising and savouring are all incorporated into this section. There are also formats for developing a less-fixed mindset and using stepped approaches to solving problems. In essence, these are all the kinds of 'happy habits' which can and do maintain overall well-being.

The resources are arranged as follows:

1. Quick focus – happy habits – identifying a series of happy habits under key headings of giving, relating, exercising, appreciating, trying out, direction, resilience, emotion, acceptance and meaning.
2. The main events helps support the identification of things that give us the most comfortable feelings and the ways in which we can try to increase these in our lives.
3. Feelings information sheet identifies the need to control feelings that may prevent us from doing what we want to do.
4. Understanding emotions helps to identify how we may feel in a range of 'negative' situations.
5. Happy habits to relieve uncomfortable feelings – using physical exercise, controlled breathing, calming pictures, reading and listening to music. The students are introduced to all of these strategies and asked to consider when and if they might use them.
6. My personal relaxation strategies encourages students to identify these.
7. Building strengths and happiness is a thought storm activity designed to initiate thinking around these areas.
8. Building strengths introduces the students to Seligman's 24 character strengths by asking for definitions of each of these in turn.
9. Strengths sort! This encourages the students to rank order their own character strengths in order and to identify those that they use the most and those that they may wish to further develop if this seems like a useful strategy.
10. Seligman's 24 character strengths part 3 – my five lowest strengths and what I can do to build them further. This activity is intended to be solution focused and enable students to identify a way forward for themselves in each of these areas.
11. Thinking about skills and strengths now and in the future again enables a self-reflection and the identification for areas of development.
12. My 10 top skills reinforces how these help both the individual and those around them.
13. Building the habit of trading skills introduces the concept and practise of trading our skills and talents.
14. The confidence habit helps to support the development of a habit which really can help to keep us well and positive in our daily lives. This

encourages the students to identify and use sources of confidence and to also analyse their own existing confidence levels.

15. Four sources of confidence supports the students in identify sources that they have in their lives including experience, encouragement, role models and the management of feelings.

16. Confidence givers and confidence takers helps students to identify these in their lives and how they can also increase the role of the confidence givers in their lives.

17. Recording my uniqueness – this is me! this provides the students with an opportunity to positively affirm who they are and what makes them a special and unique individual.

18. Brain storm – what is the respect habit – the students are asked to define respect and what they respect about themselves.

19. A motivational reflection which highlights achievements and skills and, once again, is a very 'happy' habit in terms of reinforcing the positives and overall feelings of well-being.

20. Motivate yourself is an activity which helps the student to identify their unique qualities.

21. Getting the 'healthy habit' supports students in identifying what they do in terms of utilising healthy options and strategies.

22. Getting the self-management habit focuses on the development and trial-ling of a range of anger management strategies.

23. Get the healthy habit – healthy habits and healthy options – identifying the most and least healthy options.

24. Understand that stress – true or false – distinguishing the stress facts in order to engage in healthier ways of managing this emotion and situations which can be a key cause of stress.

25. Plan and prioritise to reduce stress which provides students with a day planner format for promoting organization and time management.

26. Focus on stress – how do we cope? This helps the students to identify stressors and negative responses and to begin to react more positively to such difficulties.

27. Understanding anger – this helps to identify the positive aspects of anger and how to express this emotion in a positive way. The group thought storm approach also normalises responses and helps to support the development of a group support network – emphasising the importance of sharing strategies and self-help mechanisms.

28. Leisure pursuits – developing healthy habits and options and making leisure time more productive and enjoyable is the focus of this activity.

29. 10 core beliefs – get the self-knowledge habit! This activity engages the students in thinking more about the impact of negative core beliefs.

30. Core beliefs quiz is a self-reflection activity using a sentence completion format to distinguish between unhelpful and helpful core beliefs.

31. Reflect my thoughts and feelings diary encourages students to pinpoint situations that they may need to avoid in order to maintain happiness levels and well-being.

32. The best me is a timed writing activity which aims to support the identification of a best possible future self.

33. Relax and take 10 minutes to chill provides the student with a short relaxation strategy to practise on a regular basis.

34. Visualise your peaceful place engages the students in identifying the image of a place which enables them to truly relax and feel happy and a peace with themselves and the world that they live in.

35. My exercise diary asks the students to choose their exercise, identify time spent, feelings before and feelings after.

36. Here's how to rethink your anger! This activity is in the form of an information sheet which highlights seven easy steps to re-thinking anger as follows: recognise, empathise, think, hear, include, notice and keep attending.

37. Feelings thermometer helps students to identify how 'hot' their feelings are by utilising the visual tool or cue of a thermometer.

38. Savouring habits introduces the concept of savouring situations and helps to define this concept and to support the identification of ways in which students do savour current experiences and emphasises the value of developing such a happy habit.

39. Savouring tenses is an activity which helps the students to identify things that they can and should savour from the past present and future.

40. Three good things – Be Grateful helps to reinforce the need to practise gratitude on a regular basis.

41. Information sheet pleasure and mastery – this activity defines these two concepts and helps the students to identify the amount of pleasure and mastery they gain from an activity by using the scaling systems provided on the activity sheet.

42. Daily diary helps to support the identification of good times which can be planned out for the week ahead.

43. Is-your-mindset-fixed activity engages the students in self-reflection regarding their views as to how they might get 'better' at things on their 'bad list'.

44. Mission impossible – this activity aims to challenge fixed mind sets by finding the evidence to show that statements are false.

45. Being solution focused helps students to develop such a focus by asking them to identify and articulate 10 solutions to one specific problem.

46. A balanced view – this supports the identification of possible negative and positive consequences to one specific solution.

47. Top talk activity focuses upon identifying the support to be gained from someone else who is able to cope with a similar or the same problem to your own.

48. Traffic lights presents a stepped approach or strategy to solving problems which once again is both logical and solution focused.

49. Using the cartoon storyboard technique is another stepped approach to solving problems and can once again facilitate the process and reduce anxiety due to the security of working through the process in a consistent manner.

Part 3 Friendly habits

These activities focus on the development of friendly habits – the habits of being a good friend and adopting a 'reaching out' stance which involves caring for others and doing good in and for the community. The idea of personal responsibility for developing and maintaining such behaviours is reinforced here. One key element of building such relationships and friendly habits is the development of empathy alongside the ability to maintain a positive outlook which includes recognising and pre-empting negative automatic thoughts about ourselves and others. There is therefore an opportunity to also develop key tools and strategies from cognitive behaviour therapy (CBT). The final focus is then on the development of friendly habits which include writing letters of thanks and also in engaging in daily acts of kindness.

The resources are arranged as follows:

1. A friendly habit – saying the 'right' thing – what would you say in a range of different situations in order to show empathy to others?
2. The feeling cards again reinforce the importance of empathy and putting ourselves into another's shoes in a range of different situations.
3. The information sheet highlights the distinction between passive, aggressive and assertive communication and the importance of developing the latter in order to develop friendly habits of communication.
4. The self-checklist enables the students to measure/identify their own behaviours in both categories.
5. The information sheet encourages students to consider the use of voice, speech, facial expression, eye contact and body movements when we are submissive, aggressive and assertive.
6. A friendly habit-making positive comment activity encourages the students to be positive about themselves and those they meet and to gain an understanding as to how such responses can support them in succeeding and achieving their goals.
7. Do you listen? Identifying blocking behaviours to the listening process engages the students in further self-reflection regarding their own skills and behaviours.
8. Reflections on developing more empathy: how would you feel if? This can be conducted as a circle time activity or on an individual basis.
9. Conflict information sheet identifies three possible results of a conflict (win–win, win–lose, lose–lose) and supports students with working on top tips to aid the process of reducing conflict or making it more productive.
10. Key conflict – identifying a conflict that he/she would like to solve or sort out and working through a stepped process in order to identify a way forward.
11. Friendship quiz is a self-reflection activity in which the students are asked to identify ways in which they can further improve their skills.
12. Friendship targets – setting targets to be a better friend.

13. Friendship issues cards – working with others to identify a range of solutions to a series of friendship problems or issues.
14. And the credits go to . . . my credit list is a means of developing the habit of identifying and valuing those who love and support us.
15. Things I can do for others – the outward focus is a strategy which is very good in terms of building levels of happiness and is a thought storm activity for the group as a whole.
16. The Incredibles – this activity asks the students to identify superheroes in their family, class or group.
17. Compliments cards engages the students in formulating and then sending private compliments to others which is another way of showing gratitude to others.
18. Good friends have good listening encourages students to evaluate their own skills in this particular area and to specifically identify non-verbal behaviours that they might observe in a good listener.
19. The habit of using tools from Cognitive Behaviour Therapy (CBT) – Information sheet 1 describes the links between thinking, feeling and behaving.
20. CBT 2 provides some examples of these links and shows how negative thoughts can lead to negative feelings and behaviours and highlights the need to gain 'control' by changing how we think.
21. A good time engages the students in identifying a happy time and the thoughts, feelings and behaviours associated with this time.
22. A bad time engages the students in identifying a bad time and the thoughts, feelings and behaviours associated with this time and also prompts them to consider if they are in a negative trap in terms of their thinking patterns.
23. A good habit – breaking the negative cycle encourages the students to identify negative automatic thoughts (NATs) and shows them that is the first step needed to become a more positive person.
24. Positives and negatives – helps to identify both positive and negative thoughts that they have about themselves and their future.
25. Faulty thinking is an information sheet intended to support the identification of these behaviours in order to then be able to preempt them. This identifies six types of faulty thinking: doing down, blowing up, predicting failure, over-emotional thoughts, setting yourself up or blaming yourself.
26. How faulty is your thinking? This is a self-reflection quiz and highlights the fact that it is very important that we become fully aware of when and how we engage in these behaviours and negative thought processes/errors of thinking.
27. Information sheet – controlling thoughts – this provides information on a range of strategies to try and reduce the level of faulty thinking that we may engage in on a regular basis.
28. Test it! this helps the students to identify the negative automatic thought they have most regularly.
29. Reframing negative automatic thoughts (NATs) provides students with some examples of NATs to reframe.

30. Key questions provides the students with a process to test out negative thinking and this can be a very powerful tool for supporting more realistic thinking.

31. A letter of thanks – studies have shown that expressing gratitude to others can boost our own happiness. This activity provides the students with a proforma to write their letters to a friend or person who has positively influenced their lives.

32. Message in a bottle – writing a note to a friend to support them in the development of their skills and activities is the focus of this activity.

33. Acts of kindness – doing things to help others is not only good for the recipients – it has a positive payback for our happiness and health, too. When people experience kindness it also makes them kinder as a result – so kindness is contagious!

34. Random acts of kindness diary requires the students to record and reflect upon these daily acts using the format provided.

Section 4
The activities

Part 1 Building habits

What is a habit?

We can have both 'good' and 'bad' habits and these can affect how we live our lives and our overall well-being.

Make a list of habits that you think are good and those you consider to be bad. Discuss with others and see if there is any agreement.

Good habits	Bad habits

Do you think that some of our habits can help us to become happier people? What is a happy habit? What things do you do on a daily basis that make you experience more positive feelings?

What is happiness?

There are two major ideas of happiness and well-being.

| **Feeling good** | and | **Flourishing** |

Feeling good is about having positive feelings, experiencing pleasure and developing good relationships.

Flourishing is the result of living a good and meaningful life. You flourish when you feel that you are leading a good life and when others think you are too.

The Greek philosopher Aristotle thought that you needed to feel good and to flourish in order to achieve true happiness.

Things I can do to feel good	Things I can do to flourish
Have fun!	Develop my talents!
Challenge negative thoughts!	Be future focused!
Keep fit!	Set good goals!
Have positive relationships!	Make a positive contribution to others!

Information sheet

Happiness

We sometimes hear people saying 'My schooldays were the happiest days of my life.' But most young people will know that being at school and being dependent on their family gives them personal problems that sometimes make happiness difficult, and people who have left school know that being dependent and responsible in various ways gives them personal problems that make happiness difficult. Who is happy? Let's have a think!

STOP AND REFLECT!

1. How important are these factors in being happy?

money	having power
being young	being important or famous
good health	interesting work
good friends	love
having a car, a nice house, a fur coat	having children

Does happiness depend on factors like these? Or it depends on a person's attitude to life and his attitude to other people?

2. Does happiness come to us by accident? In what ways can we make ourselves happy? (think about those happy habits) Some people who are seriously ill appear to be happy all the time. How is that possible? Is it better not to think about being happy or unhappy?
3. What are the things in your daily life that constantly make you happy? How could you be happier than you are now?
4. Are these important factors in unhappiness?

    being without love
    having nothing to do
    being ill
    being lonely
    hurting someone else

5. Who is the happiest person you know? Why is he or she happy?
6. Is it possible to be happy without other people? Would you be happy if you lived alone in a forest or desert? What can a lonely person, for example, a widow or a divorced woman, do to make her life happy?
7. Are men and women happy in different ways and for different reasons?
8. Why do some people have a feeling of guilt when they are very happy? Is it wrong or selfish to be happy?
9. Is it important to be happy?

My happiness!

Take a moment to think about what happiness *means* to you. Record whatever comes in to your head.

What does happiness mean to you?

Example: Feeling good about how things are going

Now think about specific things that often make you happy. These could be activities, people, places or anything else that comes to mind.

What things make you happy?

Example: A relaxing day out with my best friend

Assess your happiness

(a) Your overall level of happiness with life (General Happiness Survey):
www.authentichappiness.sas.upenn.edu/tests/GeneralTest t. aspx?id=250

(b) Your current mood (Positive and Negative Affect survey, PANAS):
www.authentichappiness.sas.upenn.edu/tests/SameAnswers t.aspx?id=286

Ten habits to happier living

There are 10 habits to happier living. The first 5 focus on how we interact with the OUTSIDE world and the second 5 come from WITHIN us! Look at these 10 habits very carefully. . . .

GIVING	Do things for others
RELATING	Connect with people
EXERCISING	Take care of your body
APPRECIATING	Notice the world around
TRYING OUT	Keep learning new things
DIRECTION	Have goals to look forward to
RESILIENCE	Find ways to bounce back
EMOTION	Take a positive approach
ACCEPTANCE	Be comfortable with who you are
MEANING	Be part of something bigger

In smaller groups, discuss what you understand each of these habits to mean for you in your life. How do you think, for example, that you can get into the habit of building your resilience on a daily basis or increasing your levels of self-acceptance and direction? What are the habits you can build into you daily life?

Happiness log format

Keep a daily happiness log. Record your activities and moments when you felt happy or made others happy.

What I did	How I or others felt
7.00 a.m.	
8.00	
9.00	
10.00	
11.00	
12.00	
1.00 p.m.	
2.00	
3.00	
4.00	
5.00	
6.00	
7.00	
8.00	
9.00	
10.00	
11.00	

Acceptance cards
It's good to be you!
Be happy with yourself!

Cut out the cards and play the Acceptance Game! Work in a group of 6–8 and nominate one person to shuffle the cards and take the top card, completing the sentence or answering the question. Return the card to the bottom of the pile and continue around the group. The students can take another card or pass if necessary. Enjoy the game! (The two sheets provide 30 cards for each group.)

I'm good at . . .	To person opposite – say two things that you like about them.	I know I'm successful when . . .
I'm getting better at . . .	I know when others accept me because . . .	My best point is . . .
My main strengths are . . .	My Mum or Dad or carer thinks I'm good at . . .	My best day was . . .
I think my friends like me because . . .	I know that my Mum or Dad or carer accept me for who I am because . . .	My friends like me because . . .
I like myself because . . .	I feel positive when . . .	My best subject is . . .

I feel motivated by . . .	If you could be anyone else in the group who would it be and why?	The best bit about how I look is . . .
What is most important to me is . . .	It's Good to be You!	My greatest talent is . . .
I feel important when . . .	To person opposite what do people like about him or her?	I know I have the power to . . .
My best achievement is . . .	In this game I most respect because . . .	My best quality is . . .
To person on your right – identify two positive things about them.	I feel confident when . . .	To person on your left identify two positive things about them.

My happiness shield

Use the shield to record all the things, people, thoughts, feelings and behaviours that you have which can protect you against stress and adversity. Use your shield in such times and visualise it giving you protection. Practise this happy habit!

Identifying positive traits – a useful habit!

Kind	Insightful	Sensitive
Intelligent	Funny	Organised
Hardworking	Patient	Selfless
Loyal	Realistic	Practical
Attractive	Honest	Mature
Down-to-earth	Generous	Focused
Goofy	Modest	Courteous
Creative	Serious	Grateful
Accepting	Independent	Open-minded
Strong	Trusting	Positive
Friendly	Resilient	Responsible
Flexible	Cheerful	Cooperative
Nurturing	Self-directed	Tolerant
Thoughtful	Reliable	Innovative
Confident	Relaxed	Balanced
Optimistic	Listener	
Respectful	Brave	
Determined	Decisive	
Skilled	Enthusiastic	
Helpful	Forgiving	
Motivated	Humble	

Tick!

© 2015, *Using Positive Psychology to Enhance Student Achievement*, Tina Rae and Ruth MacConville, Routledge

The best habit – self-acceptance checklist

People who accept themselves and have good self-esteem:

- Have certain values they believe in, act on and can defend. At the same time they are secure enough to alter these, if they need to.
- Are able to act in their own best interests without excessive guilt. If they make 'mistakes', they are able to accept this and learn.
- Value themselves and see themselves as being of value to others, particularly to those with whom they associate.
- Are sensitive to the needs and feelings of others.
- View others positively, looking for the best in them.
- Remain confident in their ability to deal with problems, even when things seem to be going badly.
- Feel equal to others as a person – not superior or inferior – irrespective of the differences in abilities, backgrounds or attitudes.
- Accept praise without false modesty or rejection.
- Resist the efforts of others to dominate them or put them down.
- Accept the range of desires and feelings they experience – positive and negative. It does not follow from this that they will act on all desires and feelings.
- Do not worry unduly about the future or past.

Rate yourself against each statement on a scale of 1–10 (1 = not at all, 5 = a medium amount, 10 = totally). How do you need to develop/improve your levels of self-acceptance and self-esteem? Discuss with a partner.

A happy school?: Pupil questionnaire

1. What makes you feel happy in school?

   ....

2. What activities do you enjoy most?

   ....

3. Do you feel that the adults in school listen to the pupils' views?

   ....

4. Do you feel that the adults in the school show respect to and like the pupils?

   ....

5. What makes you feel sad in school?

   ....

6. What activities do you dislike the most?

   ....

7. What could you do to make the school a happy and healthy place?

   ....

8. What would you like the adults to do in order to make the school a happy and healthy place?

   ....

9. What would be your 'Safety Rules' for your school? (record over-leaf)

Self-reflection questions – build this habit!

Things I do well

- What activities do you do outside school? Sports? Hobbies?
- Are you a member of any school clubs?
- What is your best/favourite subject at school? Why?
- Have you ever won a medal or a prize?
- Do you help out at home? Can you cook, look after younger brothers or sisters, etc.?
- Do you enjoy any sports?
- Have you ever tried an unusual activity?
- Do you like using the computer or playing games on a PlayStation? Are there any games or activities you are really good at?
- Are you a neat and tidy person? Are you organised?
- What do you want to do when you leave school?

Good times

- What is your favourite place?
- Where do you like to go with your friends/family?
- Where do you feel safest?
- Where do you go to relax?
- Have you a special moment in your life you can remember?
- Can you remember a school trip you particularly enjoyed?
- Have you ever been anywhere special on holiday?
- What do you like to do at weekends?

Personal characteristics

- How would the person that knows/loves you best describe you?
- What do your friends like about you?
- When was the last time you helped someone?
- Is there anyone you look after or help to look after?
- Have you any pets that you care for?
- What do you like best about yourself?

Work through the questions.
Share your responses with a friend.
Could you be more positive about yourself? What happy habits can you build further in order to enjoy being you, enjoy good times and reinforce the things that you do well?

The mindfulness habit

Introduction

Mindfulness is a way of paying attention to the present moment. When we're mindful, we become more aware of our thoughts and feelings and better able to manage them.

Being mindful can boost our concentration, improve our relationships and help with stress or depression. It can even have a positive effect on physical problems like chronic pain.

Anyone can learn to be mindful. It's simple, you can do it anywhere, and the results can be life-changing.

Take 10 minutes each day to do a simple mindfulness meditation

Many of us spend much of our time focused either on the past or on the future, paying very little attention to what is happening right now.

Being mindful involves saying in the moment, spending more time noticing what's going on both inside ourselves and in our surroundings. Rather than trying to change things it involves accepting the way that things are, for better or for worse.

You can follow a free 10-day daily guided meditation on the Headspace website: www.getsomeheadspace.com

You can also download the free Headspace app here: http://www.getsomeheadspace.com/shop/headspace-meditation-app.aspx

© 2015, *Using Positive Psychology to Enhance Student Achievement*, Tina Rae and Ruth MacConville, Routledge

A mindful breathing activity
Breathing out the tension on your mountain

Sit still in a tall position
Get comfortable and then close your eyes
Let the tension float away from your fingers, toes and head
Look closely at one spot on the floor
Notice each breath as it goes in and feel that you are solid and strong
Imagine you're calmer with each breath as you watch the water travel
    down your mountain
Then stop and reflect and feel how calm you are

A mindful observation activity
Observe your thoughts to reduce stress

Sit quietly and imagine you are on the top of a big hill. Look down and see the train track picture of a train moving past. As you see each carriage go past, think of it as being one of your thoughts. If you get caught up in your thought and feel as if you've jumped onto the carriage, gently get back up to the top of the hill. Let that thought 'go' – notice it but don't get on the carriage.

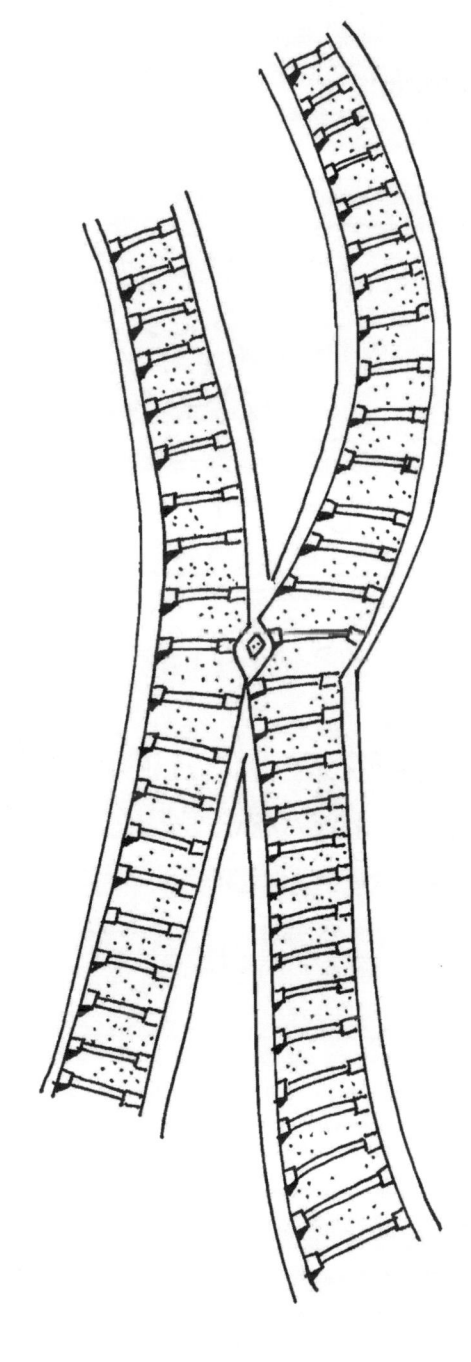

More mindful breathing

Find a comfortable place to sit, with your eyes closed and your spine as straight as you can make it.

Then focus your attention on your breathing. Be very aware of each breath as it goes in and out of your body.

When a thought or emotion pops into your head, accept it, but allow it to float on by (imagine you are pinning them to a cloud or onto a leaf floating down the river).

Focus your attention on the rise and fall of your chest, the feeling of the air entering and leaving your body.

This is mindful breathing!

Practise it!

The raisin exercise

Take one of the raisins and hold it in your hand. Look at it carefully, as if you are going to describe it to some being from another planet who has never seen one before. As best you can, be aware of thoughts or images that may sneak in as you look at this object. Simply note that they are just thoughts and return your attention to this object. Notice the colours of the object. What does the surface look like? Is it bumpy or smooth? Explore the object with your eyes and fingers. Is it dry or moist? Notice how the light shines on the object. Bring the raisin to your nose. Does it have any smells? Explore with your eyes, your fingers and your nose. Is your attention on this raisin in your hand? Then, whenever you're ready, place the raisin in your mouth. Explore the object. Do you notice your mouth watering? As best you can, keep your attention on the raisin and also watch your thoughts. Are the thoughts looking forward to swallowing the raisin and eating another or are they attending to the sensations of the one that is in your mouth? Gently bite the raisin. Taste the flavour. Slowly chew the raisin while noting every sensation. As you swallow the raisin, first note the intention to swallow it. Then feel it slide down your throat and into your tummy. Can you feel that your body is now exactly one raisin heavier than it was a few minutes ago?

Adapted from Semple and Lee (2008, pp. 78–79)

A mindful visualisation

Building the waterfall

Sometimes feelings and thoughts are uncomfortable and too difficult to focus on. Instead of getting caught up in thoughts or reacting to the negative feelings, picture yourself standing behind a waterfall of negative thoughts and feelings, allowing them to be there without reacting to them. See those thoughts and feelings as part of you but not as being all that you are.

Adapted from Teasdale, Segal, and Williams (1995).

A mindful relaxation

Close your eyes and be very still and imagine you are lying down outside in the warm sunshine.

Your body feels totally relaxed, at peace and calm.

As you lie comfortably in the soft grass, the rays of the sun are soaking into your muscles warming and relaxing your whole body.

You can feel the warmth of the sun on your legs and then let them relax.

Then you can let the muscles around your tummy relax.

Next feel the sun's rays on your shoulders and arms as you relax into the carpet of grass.

Now feel the warm sun on your face and as the sun touches it your whole face relaxes.

Then relax your forehead, your cheeks, your eyes and your mouth.

Relax, relax, relax.

Zzzzzzzzz!

3:1
The happiness ratio!

Barbara Frederickson (2009) has researched the happiness ratio. The IDEAL RATIO of positive to negative emotions on a daily basis is 3:1 of positive to negative – THIS RATIO ENSURES WELL-BEING. So, it is important to ensure that for every negative emotion you have three positive ones!!

Daily diary exercise
Keep a daily diary for one week and then record and count the positive and negative words/phrases you have used for each day's events. Try to calculate the 'happiness ratio' for each day and consider what this suggests about you and the way you live and experience your life.

Day	Positive words/ phrases	Negative words/ phrases	Happiness ratio	What does this say about me?
Sunday				
Monday				
Tuesday				
Wednesday				
Thursday				
Friday				
Saturday				

Boosting positive emotions
ACT!!

Key point to remember: you are in control and NOT the emotion!

There are many different ways of managing emotions and boosting well-being. These can be placed under three headings:

Active ones
Calming ones   ACT!!
Thinking ones

Thought-storm in your group and identify as many different interventions under each of the three headings below. An example of each has been provided.

Active techniques	Calming techniques	Thinking techniques
❑ Dancing	❑ Relaxation scripts	❑ Reframing
❑	❑	❑
❑	❑	❑
❑	❑	❑
❑	❑	❑
❑	❑	❑
❑	❑	❑
❑	❑	❑
❑	❑	❑
❑	❑	❑
❑	❑	❑
❑	❑	❑
❑	❑	❑
❑	❑	❑
❑	❑	❑

Boosting positive emotions
Positive remembering

Remembering past events, situations or people with love and affection and in a positive way is a very important way of maintaining well-being. It is particularly useful to develop the ability to transport yourself to positive past times when times get tough or challenging.

Create your Positive Memories Collage in the format below and include events, people and objects!

My Positive Memories Collage

My positive scroll

Sometimes we forget to think about the positive or good things that happen – NOT GOOD! Every evening, think of one thing (at least) that has happened that made you feel good. Record these on your positive scroll. At the end of the week LOOK at the list – now you'll know that positive things really do happen to you!

Developing grit

Develop GRIT to succeed.

How can you persevere when things get tough? What strengths can you use?

Very true (VT)   True of me (T)   Not true of me (NT)

Interests	
My interests change from year to year.	
I have been very interested in an idea or project for a short time but then I lost interest.	
I have difficulty keeping my focus on a project that takes a long time to finish.	
I often set a goal but I sometimes change my mind and choose another one.	
New ideas and new projects take my mind off previous ones.	
I become interested in new projects every few months.	

Effort	
I have achieved a goal that took me a long time.	
I have overcome setbacks to meet a challenge.	
I finish whatever I begin.	
Setbacks don't put me off.	
I am a hard worker.	
I am a careful worker.	

Adapted from Duckworth and Allred 2007

Self-reflection activity

The future

These are the things I am going to do to make my dreams and ambitions for the future come true. . .

1.

2.

3.

4.

These are the things I would like other people to do to help me to make my dreams and ambitions for the future come true . . .

1.

2.

3.

4.

Setting my goals – a good habit!

My Friendship Goal

My Education Goal

My Career Goal

My Leisure Goal

My Health Goal

My Priority Goal is

Think about your Priority Goal and ask yourself:

1. On a scale of 1 to 10 how much good will come if you achieve this goal and everything turns out well?
2. On a scale of 1 to 10 how much will your life be affected if you don't achieve this goal or things do not turn out well?

Think about it:

● If your answer to 1 is bigger than your answer to 2, it is clear you should go for it.
● If your answer to 2 is bigger than your answer to 1, think about a different goal.
● If your answers to 1 and 2 are the same, think about how you can increase the upside. Then just do it.
● If you can't think of an upside, don't do anything and think about the goal again tomorrow.

Climb the mountain

Write or draw all your goals/things you would like to do on a piece of paper. Cut them out and then arrange them on the mountain below. Place the ones that seem easiest to achieve at the bottom, the most difficult at the top and the slightly easier ones in the middle. NEXT – start with the first and easiest task – when you've achieved it, climb a little further up the mountain and try the next one. Remember – take SMALL steps to reach the TOP!

Hardest

Easiest

Change your behaviour – change your life!

Things I would like to do MORE often!
Write or draw on the chart below

Take up the challenge

My Main Challenge:

Stage 1 – My Steps to Succeed are:

❑
❑
❑
❑

Stage 2 – My Coping Self-talk is:

Stage 3 – Visualise Yourself being Successful

Repeat your coping self-talk while you imagine reaching your 1st step! Keep practising this

Stage 4 – Experiment!

Pick a time to face your fear or challenge – TRY IT OUT – take your first step and use your self-talk

Stage 5 – Reward!

Treat yourself for being successful

Don't give up! Keep going!

Break the steps down into smaller ones if you don't succeed at first!

Money facts
True or false

Consider each of the following statements and discuss in a group. Do you think they are true or false? Provide a rationale for each of your judgements.

Money always makes people happy	Having enough money to satisfy basic needs is important
Wanting more and more money can make you feel depressed	Living what you preach is more important than being rich
Having good relationships makes you happier than having money	Using money to help others will make you happy
Materialistic people are less happy than people who aren't worried about possessions	People who are well off generally experience good health
An increase in income ensures an increase in well-being	Working to achieve goals makes you happier than actually reaching them

What impacts on our happiness?

Look at each of the factors and then record your responses: YES/NO and the rationale.

Factor	Yes/No	Why
Optimism		
Self-esteem		
Being kind		
Warm climate		
Gender		
Money		
Close friends		
Marriage		
Work/job		
Children		
Sleep		
Religion		
Purpose		
Hobbies		
Education		
Winning the lottery		
Being beautiful/ famous		

Five happy habits

There are five things we can do to make ourselves happier. Look at each one and then consider and formulate a personal target and strategy for yourself under each one.

	My target	My strategy
1. Make lots of friends and be kind to them		
2. Be grateful for what you have every day		
3. Don't compare yourself badly with others		
4. Don't compare yourself to those in the media/famous personalities		
5. Savour your experiences		

Get the flow habit

Mihaly Csikszentmihalyi identified the concept of *flow* in the 1960s when he was doing research into the creative process.

He noticed how ARTISTS would ignore hunger, discomfort and tiredness when they were working on their paintings. They were 'in the flow'.

What are your 'flow' activities?

Quick focus!!
Happy habits – things we can do!

GIVING   Do things for others

Caring about others is fundamental to our happiness. Helping other people is not only good for them and a great thing to do, it also makes us happier and healthier too. Giving also creates stronger connections between people and helps to build a happier society for everyone. And it's not all about money – we can also give our time, ideas and energy. So if you want to feel good, do good!

Q: What do you do to help others?

RELATING   Connect with people

Relationships are the most important overall contributor to happiness. People with strong and broad social relationships are happier, healthier and live longer. Close relationships with family and friends provide love, meaning, support and increase our feelings of self-worth. Broader networks bring a sense of belonging. So taking action to strengthen our relationships and create new connections is essential for happiness.

Q: Who matters most to you?

EXERCISING   Take care of your body

Our body and mind are connected. Being active makes us happier as well as being good for our physical health. It instantly improves our mood and can even lift us out a depression. We don't all need to run marathons – there are simple things we can all do to be more active each day. We can also boost our well-being by unplugging from technology, getting outside and making sure we get enough sleep!

Q: How do you stay active and healthy?

APPRECIATING   Notice the world around

Ever felt there must be more to life? Well, good news: there is! And it's right here in front of us. We just need to stop and take notice. Learning to be more mindful and aware can do wonders for our well-being in all areas of life – like our walk to work, the way we eat or our relationships. It helps us get in tune with our feelings and stops us dwelling on the past or worrying about the future – so we get more out of the day-to-day.

Q: When do you stop and take notice?

TRYING OUT   Keep learning new things

Learning effects our well-being in lots of positive ways. It exposes us to new ideas and helps us stay curious and engaged. It also gives us a sense of accomplishment and helps boost our self-confidence and resilience. There are many ways to learn new things – not just through formal qualifications. We can share a skill with friends, join a club, learn to sing, play a new sport and so much more.

Q: What new things have you tried recently?

DIRECTION Have goals to look forward to

Feeling good about the future is important for our happiness. We all need goals to motivate us and these need to be challenging enough to

excite us, but also achievable. If we try to attempt the impossible this brings unnecessary stress. Choosing ambitious but realist goals gives our lives direction and brings a sense of accomplishment and satisfaction when we achieve them.

> **Q: What are your most important goals?**

RESILIENCE   Find ways to bounce back

All of us have times of stress, loss, failure or trauma in our lives. But how we respond to these has a big impact on our well-being. We often cannot choose what happens to us, but in principle we can choose our own attitude to what happens. In practise it's not always easy, but one of the most exciting findings from recent research is that resilience, like many other life skills, can be learned.

> **Q: How do you bounce back in tough times?**

EMOTION   Take a positive approach

Positive emotions – like joy, gratitude, contentment, inspiration and pride – are not just great at the time. Recent research shows that regularly experiencing them creates an 'upward spiral', helping to build our resources. So although we need to be realistic about life's up and downs, it helps to focus on the good aspects of any situation – the glass half full rather than the glass half empty.

> **Q: What are you feeling good about?**

ACCEPTANCE   Be comfortable with who you are

No one's perfect but so often we compare our insides to other people's outsides. Dwelling on our flaws – what we're not rather than what we've got – makes it much harder to be happy. Learning to accept ourselves, warts and all, and being kinder to ourselves when things go wrong, increases our enjoyment of life, our resilience and our well-being. It also helps us accept others as they are.

Q: What is the real you like?

MEANING   Be part of something bigger

People who have meaning and purpose in their lives are happier, feel more in control and get more out of what they do. They also experience less stress, anxiety and depression. But where do we find 'meaning and purpose'? It might be our religious faith, being a parent or doing a job that makes a difference. The answers vary for each of us but they all involve being connected to something bigger than ourselves.

Q: What gives your life meaning?

The main events

List the main places, people and activities in your life. Then record the feelings that go with each of these on the chart below.

Place, person/activity	Feelings

Which gives you the most comfortable feelings?
Which gives you the most uncomfortable feelings?
How can you get the happier habit of spending MOST time with those who make you feel comfortable and happier?

Feelings information sheet

You have identified some of the places you go to or things you do that produce STRONG or UNCOMFORTABLE FEELINGS.

Generally – we try to do things/go places/be with people that make us feel comfortable.

We tend to AVOID the things that make us feel uncomfortable.

The BIG BUT! Sometimes our feelings TAKE OVER and STOP us doing what we really want to do.

- You may want to go to the party but you feel so NERVOUS you can't make yourself go.
- You may want to see your friends but you feel so WORRIED about going you just can't see them.

WE NEED TO CONTROL THESE FEELINGS TO BREAK DOWN THE BARRIERS!

Learn the happy habits strategies! Try them out! Don't give up!

Understanding emotions

How do I feel when. . . . . . .

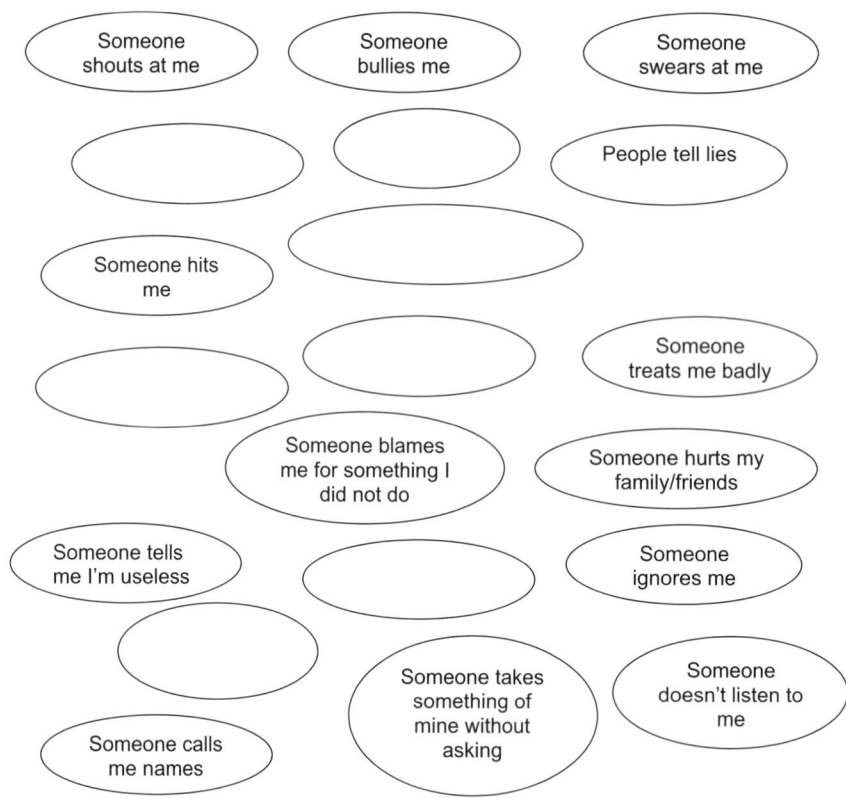

Write the emotions you experience inside the bubbles. Add some of your own experiences into the blank bubbles.

Happy habits to relieve uncomfortable feelings

Consider each of the strategies. . . . Tick against those that you think you might be able to use. When do you think each strategy might help you most?

PHYSICAL EXERCISE

A good walk, run or swim can help you to get rid of angry or anxious feelings.

☐ Yes/No

CONTROLLED BREATHING

Slowly breath in, hold for 5–10 seconds and then slowly let out the breath. As you do this, say 'RELAX' to yourself.

☐ Yes/No

CALMING PICTURES

Visualise a special place in your mind – somewhere really restful and peaceful. Turn this picture on when you feel uncomfortable.

☐ Yes/No

READING

Read a book – escape into a fantasy world to relax.

☐ Yes/No

LISTENING TO MUSIC

Listen to your favourite music – something that makes you feel happy and relaxed and takes your mind off the problem.

☐ Yes/No

Think of your own . . . what works for you apart from these?

My personal relaxation strategies

Thought-storm! What makes me relax and feel calm!

Make a **Relaxation Plan** – identify your three most stressful situations and the strategies you would now use to try to keep calmer and stay more relaxed in each situation. Try them out!

Building strengths and happiness

A strength is a positive character trait that feels authentic and energising (Linley 2008)

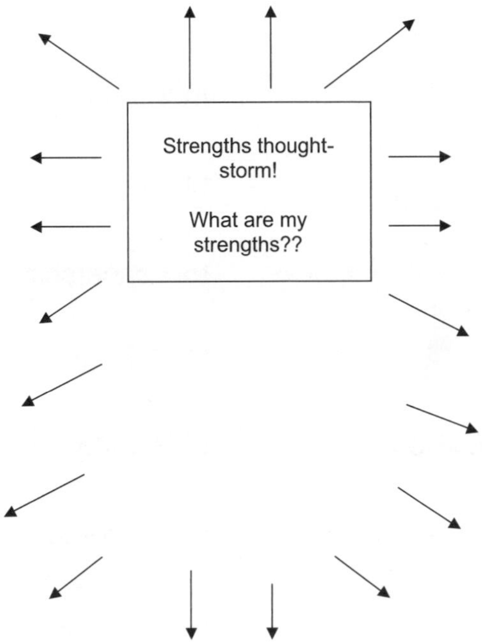

Strengths thought-storm!

What are my strengths??

Building strengths!

Seligman's 24 character strengths
Part 1
Define the strengths! Use a dictionary/Google, work with a partner and then feedback to the group.

1. Creativity	13. Citizenship
2. Curiosity	14. Fairness
3. Open-mindedness	15. Leadership
4. Love of learning	16. Forgiveness
5. Keeping perspective	17. Humility
6. Bravery	18. Prudence
7. Persistence	19. Self-regulation
8. Integrity	20. Appreciation of beauty
9. Vitality	21. Gratitude
10. Love	22. Hope
11. Kindness	23. Humour
12. Social intelligence	24. Spirituality

Strengths sort!
Seligman's 24 character strengths

Part 2

Cut out and rank order which are your greatest strengths?

Creativity	Citizenship
Curiosity	Fairness
Open-mindedness	Leadership
Love of learning	Forgiveness
Keeping perspective	Humility
Bravery	Prudence
Persistence	Self-regulation
Integrity	Appreciation of beauty
Vitality	Gratitude
Love	Hope
Kindness	Humour
Social intelligence	Spirituality

Seligman's 24 character strengths

Part 3
My five lowest strengths

Strength	Things I can do to build this
1.	
2.	
3.	
4.	
5.	

Thinking about skills and strengths now and in the future

Things I am good at . . .	Things I might be able to do with this skill in the future . . .
*	*
*	*
*	*
*	*
*	*
*	*
*	*
*	*
*	*
*	*
*	*
*	*

Think ahead! Use your skills!

My 10 top skills

Stop, Think and Reflect – Then complete the chart:

	Top skill	How this helps me	How this helps others
1.			
2.			
3.			
4.			
5.			
6.			
7.			
8.			
9.			
10.			

Building the habit of trading skills

If there was no such thing as 'money', we may have to resort to trading our skills (e.g., 'you can babysit for me and I will do 2 hours typing for you'; 'you can sew my curtains and I will make you some shelves'). What skills would you trade? What would you like in return? Complete the chart below and then discuss with others in the group.

Skills to trade	Things to give in return

The confidence habit!
Using sources of confidence – what is confidence?

Scale the definitions

1 = this is not me   3 = this is sometimes me   5 = this is always me

You feel relaxed	1	2	3	4	5
You feel secure	1	2	3	4	5
You believe in yourself	1	2	3	4	5
You don't think others are always better than you	1	2	3	4	5
You set realistic goals	1	2	3	4	5
You do as well as you can	1	2	3	4	5
You don't believe in an aggressive way/show off when you feel insecure	1	2	3	4	5
You act confident even if you don't feel like it	1	2	3	4	5
Your self-esteem levels let you make mistakes and learn from them	1	2	3	4	5
You don't always worry about what others think	1	2	3	4	5
You tend to achieve what you want	1	2	3	4	5

Four sources of confidence

1. EXPERIENCE Previous success will make you feel confident	2. ROLE MODELS Positive people who are confident will inspire you
3. ENCOURAGEMENT People who believe in you will make you feel confident	4. MANAGING FEELINGS Your ability to manage stress and cope when it goes wrong will help you to feel confident

People, places, situations and memories can all give and take away our confidence. Record your example.

CONFIDENCE GIVERS	CONFIDENCE TAKERS

Stop, think and reflect

How can you reduce the number of confidence takers in your life?

What can you do? Draw up a list of strategies to avoid the confidence takers.

This will help to build your levels of happiness! Get into the habit of surrounding yourself with those confidence givers!

Recording my uniqueness – this is me! A happy habit!

I like myself Because…

I like myself Because…

I like myself Because…

I like myself Because…

Accept and Respect Yourself

I like myself Because…

I like myself Because…

I like myself Because…

I like myself Because…

Signed _____ Date _____

Brainstorm – the respect habit

What is 'respect'? What do I respect about myself?

Work on your own at first, and then with others in the group. Do we share similar definitions of respect? Do we respect the same things about ourselves?

A motivational reflection

Look into a mirror and draw what you see. Then stop and think! Reflect upon yourself, your achievements and the skills that you have learnt to date. Record your ideas inside a drawing of a mirror.

Skills   Skills

Achievements   Achievements

Now consider one achievement in detail and answer the following questions on the reverse of this sheet:

- Why did you achieve this?
- What did you feel, think and do at the time?
- Would you do anything differently in a similar situation in the future?

Motivate yourself!

You are unique! Celebrate the difference!

In all the world there is nobody quite like you! There are people who are different and people who are similar but nobody is exactly the same, with the same thoughts, ideas, feelings, behaviours, dreams, words, hopes, fantasies and appearance. Stop for a time and reflect upon these areas – jot down some notes in each box.

A unique thought	A unique feeling	A unique fear
A unique hope	A unique fantasy	A unique dream
A unique appearance	A unique word or statement	A unique idea

There may be some things that you'd like to change in the future. Try to identify one or two of these and then work out how you might effect such a change and who will help and support you in doing this.

© 2015, *Using Positive Psychology to Enhance Student Achievement*, Tina Rae and Ruth MacConville, Routledge

Getting the healthy habit – which is healthy?

Tick against the things you like to do. Then talk it through with the rest of your class. How healthy are your behaviours?

Eat an apple ✓ ✗ ☐ ☐	Play the computer/ go on line ✓ ✗ ☐ ☐	Eat a packet of crisps ✓ ✗ ☐ ☐
Play football ✓ ✗ ☐ ☐	Run/go to the gym ✓ ✗ ☐ ☐	Watch TV ✓ ✗ ☐ ☐
Eat vegetables ✓ ✗ ☐ ☐	Reframe negative thoughts ✓ ✗ ☐ ☐	Use self-calming strategies ✓ ✗ ☐ ☐
Spend time with people who love you ✓ ✗ ☐ ☐	Read a book ✓ ✗ ☐ ☐	Think positive and keep trying ✓ ✗ ☐ ☐
Have a bath/shower ✓ ✗ ☐ ☐	Clean your teeth ✓ ✗ ☐ ☐	Have a fizzy drink ✓ ✗ ☐ ☐

Getting the self-management habit! Anger management skills to try out!

Recognise your anger early	If you're yelling, it's probably too late. Learn the warning signs that you're getting angry so you can change the situation quickly. Some common signs are feeling hot, raising voices, balling of fists, shaking and arguing.
Take a timeout	Temporarily leave the situation that is making you angry. If other people are involved, explain to them that you need a few minutes alone to calm down. Problems usually aren't solved when one or more people are angry.
Deep breathing	Take a minute to just breathe. Count your breaths – four seconds inhaling, four seconds holding your breath, and four seconds exhaling. Really keep track of time, or you might cheat yourself! The counting helps take your mind off the situation as well.
Exercise	Exercise serves as an emotional release. Chemicals released in your brain during the course of exercise create a sense of relaxation and happiness.
Express your anger	Once you've calmed down, express your frustration. Try to be assertive, but not confrontational. Expressing your anger will help avoid the same problems in the future.
Think of the consequences	What will be the outcome of your next anger-fuelled action? Will arguing convince the other person that you're right? Will you be happier after the fight?
Visualisation	Imagine a relaxing experience. Think of every sense. What do you see, smell, hear, feel and taste? Maybe you're on a beach with sand between your toes and waves crashing in the distance. Spend a few minutes imagining every detail of your relaxing scene.

© 2015, *Using Positive Psychology to Enhance Student Achievement*, Tina Rae and Ruth MacConville, Routledge

Get the keep healthy habit
Healthy options

Cut out these statements and then sort them into order in terms of the most healthy options and least healthy options.

Taking regular exercise	Not eating junk food
Going to lots of parties	Unprotected sex
Sleeping for 7–9 hours a night	Feeling happy
Low self-esteem	Feeling confident
Eating a 'proper' breakfast	Enjoying hobbies
Eating fruit and vegetables	Having lots of money
Not smoking or taking drugs	Liking other people
Eating a high fat diet	Being optimistic
Not eating sweets or too much sugar	Eating at regular times
Having good friends	Going on holiday
Eating fibre each day	Being able to relax
A low fat diet	A high fat diet
Being the 'right' weight for your height	Not getting anxious about things

Compare your sequence with a friend. Do you agree on what constitutes a healthy life-style? Can you justify your ideas?

Understand that stress! True or false?

What do we know about stress? Is it true or false?

Can we agree? Work through the following STRESS FACTS and colour-code each statement. Red = false, green = true

Stress is different for each individual.	Being unfit causes more stress and doing exercise can help you cope better.
Not keeping a balance between work and play can cause stress.	Talking and sharing your feelings can help to solve stress related problems.
Learning to relax can help to reduce stress.	Death or loss causes everyone involved stress.
Family fights or rows cause stress.	Exams cause stress but being organised and planning ahead can reduce this.
Being bullied is a stressor for most students in school.	Too much work causes stress.
Not having enough money causes stress.	People can get physical symptoms when they get stressed.
Stress is when you can't cope and feel insecure or helpless.	Solving problems by using step-by-step plans can help reduce stress.
Being organised is a good stress management strategy.	Acting aggressively can increase stress and make stressful situations worse.
Being healthy can reduce stress.	Some stress can be managed whilst other stress can be eliminated.

Plan and prioritise to reduce stress

Plan your day and manage your time.

List the things you want to achieve tomorrow	My day's plan
1.	7.00 a.m.
	8.00 a.m.
2.	9.00 a.m.
	10.00 a.m.
3.	11.00 a.m.
	12.00 a.m.
4.	1.00 p.m.
	2.00 p.m.
5.	3.00 p.m.
	4.00 p.m.
6.	5.00 p.m.
	6.00 p.m.
7.	7.00 p.m.
	8.00 p.m.
8.	9.00 p.m.
	10.00 p.m.
9.	11.00 p.m.
	midnight
10.	

Can you design your own system or means of prioritising? Have a go. Try it out and feedback to the rest of the group.

Focus on stress
How do we cope?

Identify six common types of stress that students experience both in and out of school. Then complete the following chart, working out both positive and negative reactions to these situations. An example is provided.

The Stressor	Positive Reaction	Negative Reaction
You have been off sick and you've missed a lot of work. The subject teachers are getting at you to complete it all. You feel you can't cope.	✓ Talk to a friend ✓ Tell your mum/dad/carer ✓ Make a proper timetable ✓ Keep to your timetable ✓ Ask for help	✗ Don't go into school ✗ Lie to yourself ✗ Don't ask for help ✗ Go out with friends and don't bother
1.		
2.		
3.		
4.		
5.		
6.		

Understanding anger

Write your answers to each of the questions around each shape.

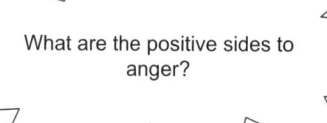

What are the positive sides to anger?

What could happen if you don't express anger?

What should you do to deal with anger positively?

Leisure pursuits – developing healthy habits and options!

Football

Partying

Social networking

Cooking

Record your leisure pursuits on the chart below.

Then rank order each one – placing the most important one first and the least important last. Then identify the most and least healthy pursuits and consider how you might make your leisure time more productive and enjoyable.

Leisure activity	Rank order	Healthy/not?

Compare your responses with a friend and highlight any similarities and differences.

10 core beliefs – get the self-knowledge habit!

What do you THINK about YOURSELF?
WHO ARE YOU?

1. I think I am
2. I think I am
3. I think I am
4. I think I am
5. I think I am
6. I think I am
7. I think I am
8. I think I am
9. I think I am
10. I think I am

Stop, think and reflect!

How do your beliefs make you FEEL?
How do your beliefs affect how you ACT?
Do NEGATIVE core beliefs set you up to fail and limit what you do?

Core beliefs quiz

Have a go at this quiz! What do you think will happen in each situation?
Stop, think and reflect and then TALK it through.

IF. . . . . THEN . . . .
If I am bad then
If I get it wrong then
If I work hard then
If I am kind then
If I have friends then
If I am good then
If I make people feel good then
If I don't have friends then
If I let people down then
If I think positively then
Which beliefs are HELPFUL? Why?
Which beliefs are UNHELPFUL? Why?

Reflect!
My thoughts and feelings diary

Day and time	The Situation Where, when and who with?	Thoughts Which were 'hot' (i.e., the strongest)?	Feelings How were you feeling?

Reflect on this diary and try to identify the triggers to the less comfortable and difficult feelings you experienced. What skills, strategies and healthy habits might you be able to use in order to cope more effectively or perhaps even avoid or alter the situation or your response to it?

The best me – timed writing activity!

Take 20 minutes to record your ideas – what would be your best possible future self in all areas of your life – home, school, career, friends, family, etc.?

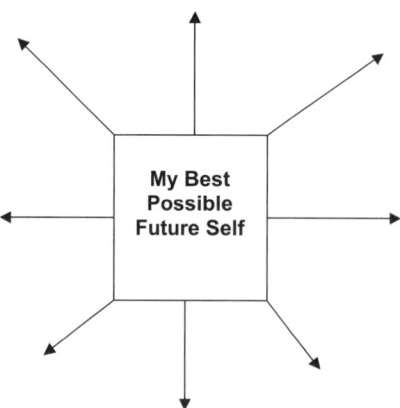

Repeat this exercise on a daily basis for one week and then consider the impact upon your happiness levels.

Relax! Take 10 minutes to chill!

Tense each of the major muscle groups in your body for about 5–10 seconds and then RELAX. Be aware that some parts of your body may be more tense than others so pay more attention to these! PRACTISE this technique!

Step 1:   Choose a quiet, warm and comfortable place
Step 2:   Sit in a comfy chair or lie on your bed
Step 3:   Make sure you won't be disturbed
Step 4:   Tense and then relax your muscles in

(a) right foot
(b) entire right leg
(c) left foot
(d) entire left leg
(e) right hand
(f) entire right arm
(g) left hand
(h) entire left arm
(i) abdomen
(j) chest
(k) neck and shoulders
(l) face

Step 5:   REPEAT
Step 6:   Close your eyes and count slowly to 100

Visualise your peaceful place

Close your eyes and visualise your most peaceful place – what does it look, feel, smell and sound like?

Reconstruct this image in your mind and then record it in images, or words (or both) below:

My exercise diary

Psychological and mental benefits of exercise include better overall well-being; better body image; increased self-esteem and confidence; lower anxiety, depression and stress levels. Physical benefits include a reduction in obesity, cardiovascular disease, heart disease, strokes, diabetes (type 2), high blood pressure and some cancers.

SO KEEP ON MOVING! Find out what exercise suits you and motivates you: dance, gym, football, etc. Then work out a weekly timetable and complete the exercise diary below:

	My exercise of choice	Time	Feelings before	Feelings after
Monday				
Tuesday				
Wednesday				
Thursday				
Friday				
Saturday				
Sunday				

Information sheet
Here's how to RETHINK your anger!

Anger is NOT something that is outside your control!

RETHINK

your anger means following these seven steps:

Recognise that you feel angry and ask yourself why you feel this way

Empathise. This means not being blinded by angry feelings but try to see how things look and feel from the other person's point of view. This is simple to do, just put yourself in the other person's shoes.

Think about your situation in a different way, especially one that offers you an alternative to just being angry.

Hear the underlying message of what the other person is trying to say to you.

Include respect and love in what you say and do even when you are angry.

Notice what happens in your body when you feel angry and notice how you can control your body to help you to calm down.

Keep your attention on the here and now and not on the past or on the future. Focus on how the problem that has made you angry can be solved.

Feelings thermometer

Where would you place the feelings you have identified on the feelings thermometer? Would anger or fury be at −100, and would the strongest positive emotions include elation/exhilaration? What would you place in the middle? Use the list of prompt words alongside your own thought-storm.

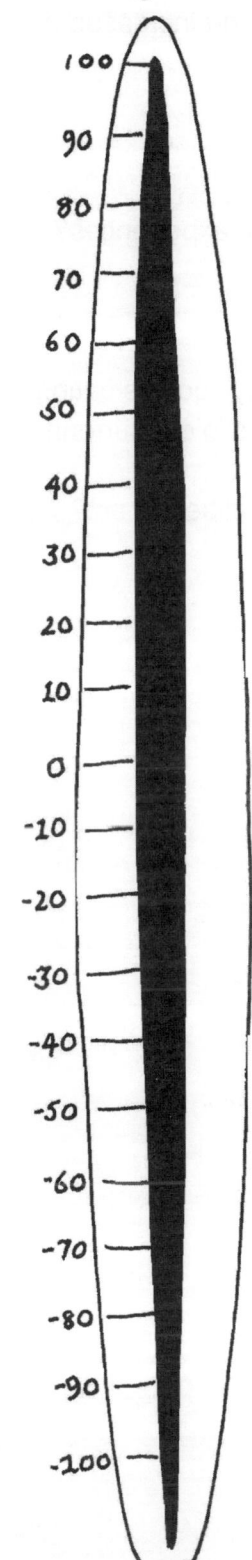

Prompt List

hopeless	annoyed
excited	tired
worried	enthusiastic
defiant	mellow
anxious	peaceful
eager	calm
carefree	receptive
depressed	exhausted
confident	optimistic
stressed	stimulated
passive	astonished
serene	engaged
frustrated	furious
noble	envious
jealous	proud
relieved	hurt
sad	incensed
at ease	fearful
kind	content
thoughtful	angry
happy	delighted

Savouring habits! Savouring situations

What is savouring? Bryant and Veroff (2007) define savouring as any thoughts or behaviours capable of 'generating, intensifying and prolonging enjoyment'.

Martin Seligman (2003) says that the ability to savour the positive experiences we have is one of the most important elements of happiness. Savouring situations fosters positive emotions and increases our overall well-being.

Questions to consider

What are your most enjoyable activities?

How frequently do you STOP AND SAVOUR these experiences?

How do you savour these activities?

When do you savour these activities?

What presents you from savouring?

Why do we sometimes just 'rush through' an activity such as eating?

Why do we not take the time to simply stop and take in our surroundings?

Why do you think we have to make 'savouring' a deliberate act?

Savouring tenses!

Think about and record the things you have savoured in the past, things you can savour now and things that you can savour in the future. Record these on the chart below and then SAVOUR!

Things I can savour from the PAST	Things I can savour NOW	Things I can savour in the FUTURE
e.g., holidays, time spent with friends/family, early childhood, etc.	e.g., friends, food, books, movies, hobbies, etc.	e.g., career, relationships, friends, holidays, exam/work success, etc.

© 2015, *Using Positive Psychology to Enhance Student Achievement*, Tina Rae and Ruth MacConville, Routledge

Three good things
Be grateful!!

Being grateful is about much more than just saying thank you – it's about not taking things for granted and having a sense of appreciation and thankfulness for life.

People who are grateful tend to be happier, healthier and more fulfilled. Being grateful can help people cope with stress and can even have a beneficial effect on heart rate.

Each day write down three good things that happened. They can be anything you feel good about or grateful for.

Even on a bad day there are normally some things that we can feel good about. Taking time to be grateful is not about ignoring the bad things – it just helps us focus our attention more on the positive, rather than dwell on the negative.

To get used to the idea, start by filling in the boxes below to describe three good things that happened to you *yesterday* and why they were good.

Try to include *why* you felt each of the things was really good.

Good Thing 1
Example: Best night's sleep for ages so felt much more energetic!
Good Thing 2
Example: Lunch with Steve and Jane – great to see good pals again.
Good Thing 3
Example: Home in time to talk to Mum. We really had fun together.

Now repeat this activity *at the end of each day* for a week. Use the blank boxes on the following pages to write down your Three Good Things down each day.

Information sheet pleasure and mastery

It can be useful to think of the amount of pleasure and mastery that good times give you. This is especially true if you have been feeling down.

PLEASURE means the amount that you enjoy doing something.

MASTERY means the amount of satisfaction that you get from the challenge of doing something.

The amount of pleasure or mastery that you get from anything is a matter of personal opinion. You can judge the amount of pleasure that you get from doing something fun by using our pleasure-ometer. You can judge the amount of mastery that you get from doing something fun by using our mastery-ometer.

Pleasure-ometer

10 Maximum Pleasure!!!

9 Loads of
8 Pleasure

7
6 Medium
5 Pleasure
4

3 Mild
2 Pleasure

1 Minimum Pleasure

Pleasure and mastery

Mastery-ometer

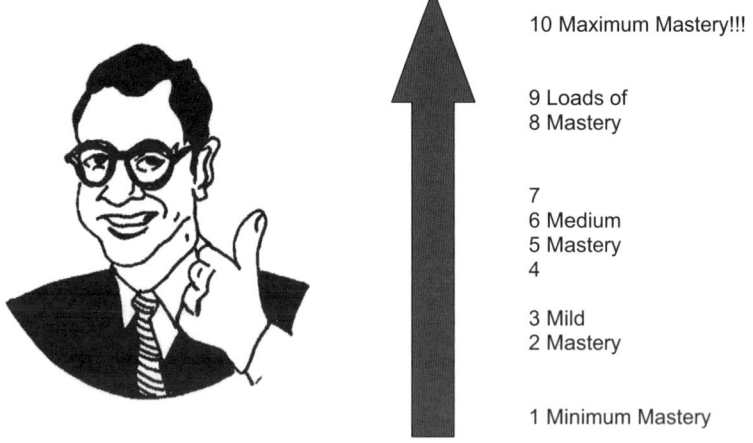

10 Maximum Mastery!!!

9 Loads of
8 Mastery

7
6 Medium
5 Mastery
4

3 Mild
2 Mastery

1 Minimum Mastery

Use a daily diary format to plan as many good times as possible over the next week.

At the end of every day rate each of your good times on our pleasure-ometer and on our mastery-ometer.

Daily diary

Good times

Use this diary to plan as many good times as possible over the next week – times when you have lots of pleasure and lots of mastery!

	Mon-day	Tues-day	Wednes-day	Thurs-day	Fri-day	Satur-day	Sun-day
9.00 a.m. 11.00 a.m.							
1.00 p.m. 3.00 p.m.							
5.00 p.m. 7.00 p.m.							
9.00 p.m. 11.00 p.m.							

Is your mindset fixed?

Make a list of things you are GOOD at and things you are BAD at. Then consider the questions below.

Things I am GOOD at. . . .	Things I am BAD at. . . .

- Do you think you can get even better at the things you are good at?
- Do you think you will always be good at the things you are good at now?
- What would happen if you failed at any of these good skills/activities?
- Have you always been bad at the things you have listed on your Bad list?
- Do you think you can get better at any of the things on your Bad list?
- What might be preventing you?
- What might help you to get better at these things?

Mission impossible

Look at the statements below and find the evidence to show that they are FALSE! For example, Richard Branson came bottom of his class, was dyslexic and left school at 16 but he is now a world renowned multi-millionaire businessman. Find someone who shows the statement to be false!

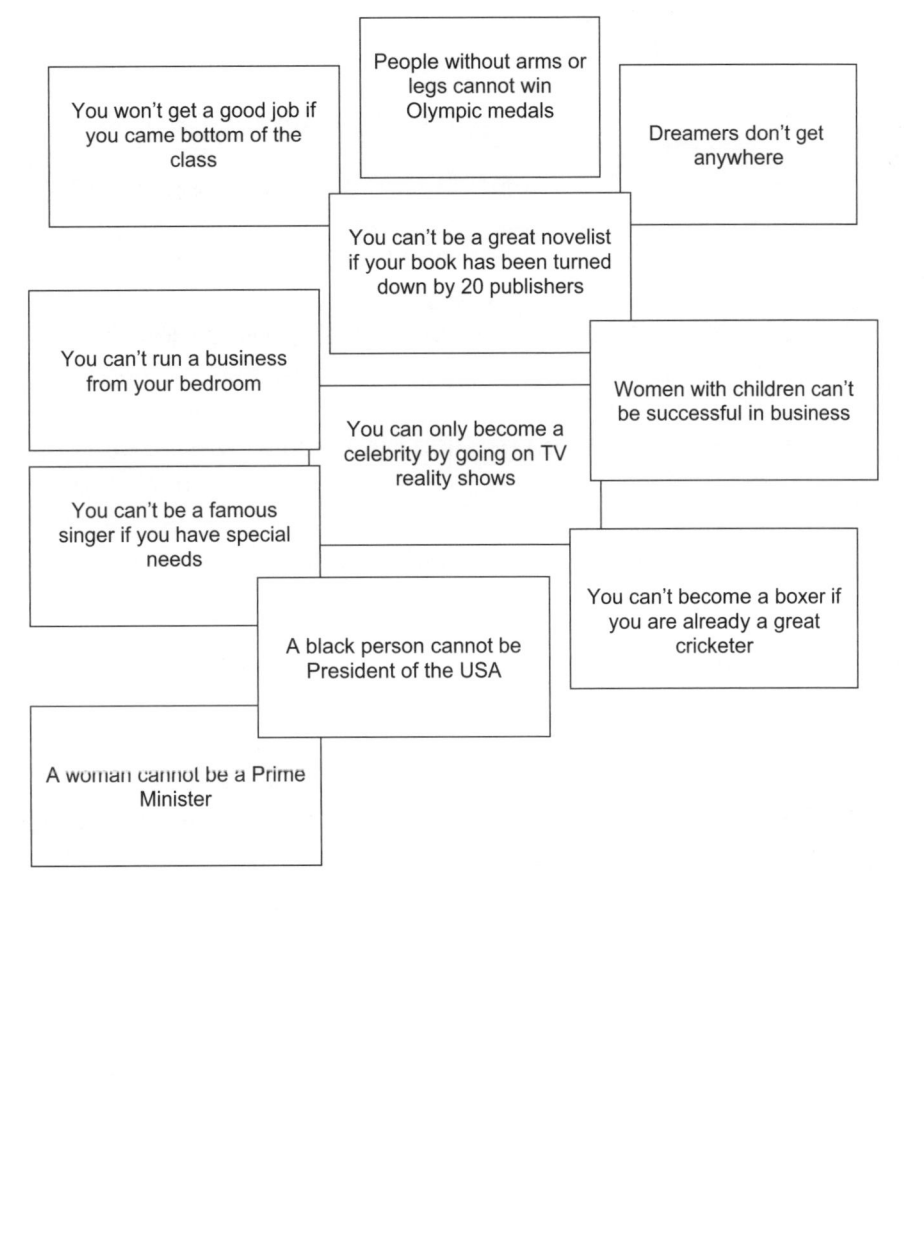

People without arms or legs cannot win Olympic medals

You won't get a good job if you came bottom of the class

Dreamers don't get anywhere

You can't be a great novelist if your book has been turned down by 20 publishers

You can't run a business from your bedroom

Women with children can't be successful in business

You can only become a celebrity by going on TV reality shows

You can't be a famous singer if you have special needs

You can't become a boxer if you are already a great cricketer

A black person cannot be President of the USA

A woman cannot be a Prime Minister

Being solution focused – focus on solutions

The problem is _____

_____

_____

_____

List all the ways you could SOLVE this problem:
I could solve this by. . .

1.

2.

3.

4.

5.

6.

7.

8.

9.

10.

NEXT STEP Ask someone else how you could solve the problem. Record their ideas on the reverse of the sheet.

A balanced view

Write down a key problem and list all the solutions you have worked on. THINK AHEAD! What would be the positive and negative consequences of each solution? Complete the consequences chart below.

Solution	Positive consequences	Negative consequences

NOW – STOP, THINK & REFLECT! Look at the consequences and make your decision. Which SOLUTION would be the best one for your particular problem?

Top talk – helping others

When you keep experiencing the same problem, find someone else who copes with it! Talk through their strategies and steps to success! Answer the following QUESTIONS:

- What is this problem?
- Who has successfully coped with this problem?
- How do they do this?
- When can I discuss their plan?
- What will my own plan then look like and when will I try it out?
- How will I reward myself for being successful?

Traffic lights

Use the Stepped Approach to solving your problems

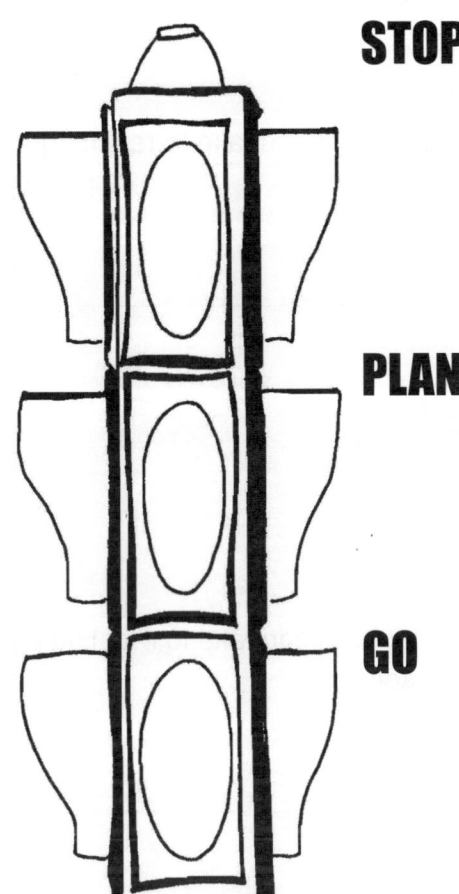

STOP   How does it look?
How do you feel?
How do you

PLAN   What are your solutions?
Which is the best one and why?
When will you try it out?

GO   Do the experiment?
Try it out
Reward yourself
Evaluate and re-plan!
Don't give up!

Using cartoon storyboard technique

This technique was created by Henry and Mayle in 2002 (see Boniwell and Ryan 2012) and is a visual tool to develop a vision of a desired outcome and identify and problem solve around any obstacles to this. Use the SIX BOXES below to solve the problems/overcome the obstacles to meeting your goal.

1. My goal and the problems/ obstacles to reaching it.	2. Step (1) I can take to reaching a solution.
3. Step (2) I can take to reaching a solution.	4. Step (3) I can take to meeting a solution.
5. Step (4) I can take to meeting a solution.	6. How I would feel if I overcame the problems and reached my goal.

A friendly habit – saying the 'right' thing!
What would you say?

Sometimes it can be quite hard to find the words needed to empathise with someone else. Look at the following statements and try to think what you would say in order to show empathy for each person. Write your response in the speech bubbles.

"I'm so rubbish at writing. I may as well not even try. I feel so dumb!"

"My dad has grounded me for smoking. It's so unfair when he smokes himself."

"I'm so ugly. I feel that I need plastic surgery or I'll never get a girlfriend."

"That teacher has just got it in for me. I keep getting into trouble and it's not my fault. She just wants me out."

"My mum keeps on saying how disappointed she is in me for getting excluded. She says I'm bad, I feel so fed up, it's all useless."

Feeling Cards

How do they feel?
How would you feel?

Beyoncé singing to an adoring audience.	The Prime Minister being booed at a conference.	An old lady being mugged.
A traveller girl being beaten up.	A young woman walking home alone late at night.	An old man peering through the curtain at a gang outside.
A miner in a tunnel.	A disabled teenager watching a football match.	A new pupil.
A young teacher having difficulties controlling the class.	A shopkeeper being racially abused.	A child at a funeral.
A girl pushing off a boy.	A boy watching two others smoking a joint.	A refugee watching other kids playing football.
Two drunk girls falling over a pram in the street.	A suicide bomber walking through a crowd.	A fat boy being bullied.
A Muslim girl having her veil pulled off by a boy.	Two gay men holding hands.	A man who has been beaten up after a night at the pub.
A girl in a new BMW.	Someone getting married.	A young girl whose parents/carers are fighting.

Information sheet
Passive, aggressive and assertive communication
Developing friendly habits!

Passive communication

When using passive communication, an individual does not express their needs or feelings. Passive individuals often do not respond to hurtful situations, and instead allow themselves to be taken advantage of or to be treated unfairly.

Traits of passive communication:

- Poor eye contact
- Allows others to infringe upon their rights
- Soft-spoken
- Allows others to take advantage

Aggressive communication

Aggressive communicators violate the rights of others when expressing their own feelings and needs. They may be verbally abusive to further their own interests.

Traits of aggressive communication:

- Use of criticism, humiliation and domination
- Frequent interruptions and failure to listen to others
- Easily frustrated
- Speaking in a loud or overbearing manner

Assertive communication

With assertive communication an individual expresses their feelings and needs in a way that also respects the rights of others. This mode of communication displays respect for each individual who is engaged in the exchange.

Traits of assertive communication:

- Listens without interrupting
- Clearly states needs and wants
- Stands up for personal rights
- Good eye contact

Aggressive or assertive? Check yourself out!

Use this self checklist honestly and see whether you are Aggressive or Assertive.

Tick the behaviour you use most often and see how you really react!

You are being assertive when you	You are being Aggressive when you
➢ 'Listen' to what others say	➢ Are 'loud'
➢ Are upfront with others when it comes to your thoughts and feelings	➢ Tend to 'do' people down either physically or verbally.
➢ Are honest with yourself when it comes to how you think and feel	➢ Get others to feel bad or upset
➢ Think of others and how they feel	➢ Don't really think about how others feel as long as you get your own way
➢ Ask confidently for what you want	➢ Put others down
➢ Are responsible for both your behaviour and what you do	➢ Get others to do what you want – even when they don't want to
➢ Don't need other people to think you're 'good'	➢ Don't listen to other people's point of view
➢ You think well of yourself and others	
➢ Acknowledge your rights and those of others	

STOP, THINK & REFLECT
What can you do to improve your skills? Who can help you?

Information sheet – Assert yourself!

	Voice	Speech	Facial expression	Eye contact	Body movements
S u b m i s s i v e	Sometimes wobbly Tone may be singsong or whining Over-soft or over-warm Often dull and in monotone Quiet, often dropping away at end	Rather uncertain, hesitant and filled with pauses Jerky, changes from fast to slow Frequent throat clearing	Unreal smile when showing anger, or being criticised Eyebrows raised in anticipation (of being rebuked etc.) Quick-changing features/ expressions	Evasive Looking down	Hand-wringing Hunched shoulders Stepping back Covering mouth with hand Nervous movements which detract (shrugs and shuffles) Arms crossed for protection
A g g r e s s i v e	Very firm, no nonsense way of speaking Tone may be sarcastic and cold Can sound hard and sharp Very harsh, often shouting, and rising at the end	Fluent, few hesitancies Often abrupt and clipped Emphasis on blaming listener Often very fast	Smile may become 'smirking' Scowls when angry Eyebrows raised in amazement/ disbelief Jaw set firm and hard Chin thrust forward	Tries to stare down and dominate Glaring and 'cold'	Finger-pointing Fist thumping Sits upright or leans forward Stands upright with head 'in the air' Strides around impatiently Arms crossed ('don't even try to come closer)
A s s e r t i v e	Steady, firm and unhur-ried Tone is warm, mid-dle range and easy to listen to Sincere and clear Neither too loud nor too quiet	Fluent with few hesitancies Empha-sis on key words Steady, calm delivery	Smiles when pleased Frowns when angry Face 'open' Fea-tures very steady – no wobbling! Jaw relaxed, but not 'loose'	Firm but not engaging in 'stare down'	Open hand movements (inviting other person to speak) 'Measured pace' hand movements (no sudden ones) Sits upright or relaxed (not slouching or cowering) Stands with head straight and relaxed in posture

Reflect: When have you behaved in a submissive, aggressive or asser-tive way? Which behaviours achieved you the best or worst outcomes for you and why?

A friendly habit – making positive comments

Look positive   Speak positive   Act positive

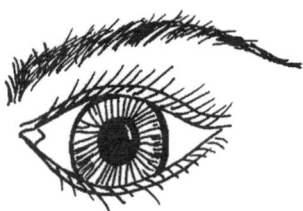  

Be positive about yourself and about the people you meet. Your attitude will help you to succeed and achieve the goals. You will also ensure that others feel positive about themselves!

Make a positive comment about:

a. The person on your left
b. The person on your right
c. The person opposite you

Then ask each person to write their response in the response box.

Positive comment	Response
a.	
b.	
c.	

Questions to discuss and think about

- How did each person respond to receiving a compliment? For example, smiling, happy, fidgeting, looking away, embarrassed.
- What is a good response to receiving a positive compliment?
- What would not be a good response and why?
- Can you 'act out' both kinds of responses, for example, a poor response might include fidgeting, looking away or denying the compliments and so on.

Do you listen?
Blocking behaviours

Do you listen to others or do you block communication? Reflect on your listening behaviours over the week and try and complete the chart below (use a tick)

	Frequently	Often	Sometimes	Not often	Not at all
Put downs (making others feel down, bad or hurt)					
Self-talk (talking about yourself and not being interested in others)					
I know best (telling others what they should or shouldn't do)					
Cutting across (interrupting)					
Interpreting (judging them and trying to put words in their mouths)					

Which blocking behaviour did you use the most?

_____

Which didn't you use?

_____

How can you become a better listener?

_____

I could . . .

_____

Reflections on developing more empathy
How would you feel if . . .

Talk in a Circle Time or class discussion about each statement and then say how you would feel (and why) if . . .

- You were the only black child in your class.
- You were mixed race.
- You were paralysed from the waist down and unable to walk.
- You didn't have nice clothes.
- You were really poor.
- You were really rich.
- Your sister had cerebral palsy.
- No one spoke your language at school.
- You couldn't read or write as well as the other kids in your class.
- You didn't have any friends.
- You were the only person in your class who believed in God and practised your religion.

Can you think of three more?

-
-
-

Think how you might cope best in three of these situations!

-
-
-

Conflict information sheet

There are three possible results of a conflict:

Win
Win

The people involved will sort out the problem without any aggression. Nobody gets hurt. A compromise is found. Both people respect themselves and each other.

Win
Lose

One person uses aggression or one person gives in. One person will get hurt. One person will get their own way.

Lose
Lose

Both people disrespect themselves and each other. Both people will resort to aggression. There is physical and emotional hurt for all concerned. Things end up worse than they originally were. Both people disrespect themselves and each other. Nobody is a winner.

Top tips for solving conflicts
Can you add any of your own?

- Listen
- Take turns to talk
- Get some help
- Compromise
- Wait
- Use 'I' messages

Share your ideas in a group. Do you agree with others' view? If so, why?

© 2015, *Using Positive Psychology to Enhance Student Achievement*, Tina Rae and Ruth MacConville, Routledge

Key conflict
Think! Analyse! Reflect!

Problem-solve! Complete the sheet and move forwards!

A conflict I'd like to sort out is:	The other person involved is:
This conflict makes me feel (tick against feeling): sad depressed worried upset stressed confused scared rejected sad fed-up frustrated angry ashamed disappointed surprised	**The other person probably feels** (tick against feeling): sad depressed worried upset stressed confused scared rejected sad fed-up frustrated angry ashamed disappointed surprised
What I want is:	What the other person wants is:
What I might do about this conflict is:	What the other person might do about this conflict is:

Some things I could do now to improve this situation:

1. _____

2. _____

3. _____

4. _____

5. _____

Friendship quiz

Stop, think and reflect!

How are your friendship skills?

Rate yourself honestly! What kind of friend are you? How are your skills? Rate yourself against each statement

1 = not a lot, 3 = sometimes, 5 = always

Statement	My rating				
1. I can listen properly to my friends.	1	2	3	4	5
2. I don't judge them.	1	2	3	4	5
3. I respect their views and feelings.	1	2	3	4	5
4. I am honest with them about my views and feelings.	1	2	3	4	5
5. I can tell my friends that I don't agree with them.	1	2	3	4	5
6. I don't talk about them behind their backs.	1	2	3	4	5
7. I don't put them down.	1	2	3	4	5
8. I try not to take my problems out on them.	1	2	3	4	5

Friendship quiz (cont.)

9. I can recognise and empathise with how they are feeling. 1 2 3 4 5

10. I can motivate my friends to do their best. 1 2 3 4 5

11. I can support them with they feel down. 1 2 3 4 5

12. I don't try to push my friends into doing what I want to do. 1 2 3 4 5

13. I can respect that they are different to me in some ways. 1 2 3 4 5

14. I can cope with the fact that they might need to be on their own sometimes. 1 2 3 4 5

15. I can cope with the fact that they have other friends. 1 2 3 4 5

Stop and think!

Can you be a better friend?
Where are your strongest skills?
Where do you need to improve your skills?

Friendship targets

Commit to being a better friend. Set your personal friendship targets.
   I will be a better friend by:

1.

2.

3.

4.

I will know that I have met my targets because. . .

. . . .
. . . .
. . . .
. . . .
. . . .
. . . .
. . . .
. . . .
. . . .
. . . .
. . . .
. . . .
. . . .
. . . .
. . . .

Signed . . . . Date . . . .

Friendship issues cards

Issue (1) Your friend can never compromise when you have an argument, he always has to 'win'.	Issue (2) Your friend thinks he's gay and has told you not to tell anyone else as he feels nervous about this.	Issue (3) Your friend's dad is always putting her down and making her feel stupid and thick.
Issue (4) Your friend recently lost his grandfather. He is feeling very down and rejecting support from friends.	Issue (5) Your friend has become more fundamentalist since 9/11 and now doesn't want to go around with non-Muslims.	Issue (6) Your friend's mum is a racist and won't have you in her house because you are black.
Issue (7) Your friend is drinking too much and having unprotected sex when she's drunk at parties.	Issue (8) Your friend is getting stressed about exams because he thinks he won't be able to pass any of them as he's not as clever as you.	Issue (9) Your friend thinks it's okay to two-time his girlfriend.
Issue (10) Your friend is really possessive and doesn't want you to have a close relationship with anyone else.	Issue (11) Your friend enjoys smoking cannabis but you don't.	Issue (12) Your friend makes jokes about people with disabilities. Your younger brother has cerebral palsy.
Issue (13) Your friend is always borrowing money from you and others and never pays it back.	Issue (14) Your friend always buys the same clothes as you and can't seem to develop her own individual style.	Issue (15) Your friend thinks girls are only good for sex and that they can't be good friends like boys.

Stop, think and reflect!

How would you solve these friendship issues? Work in small groups, share your ideas and agree on Plans of Action. Feedback to the whole group.

And the credits go to . . .
My credit list

Think of all the people who have helped and supported you. Write a list of credits, identifying what they did to help you.

Name	What they did to support/help me

Write notes of thanks to one or all of these people! Show them your gratitude for their kindness.

Things I can do for others

Write and draw

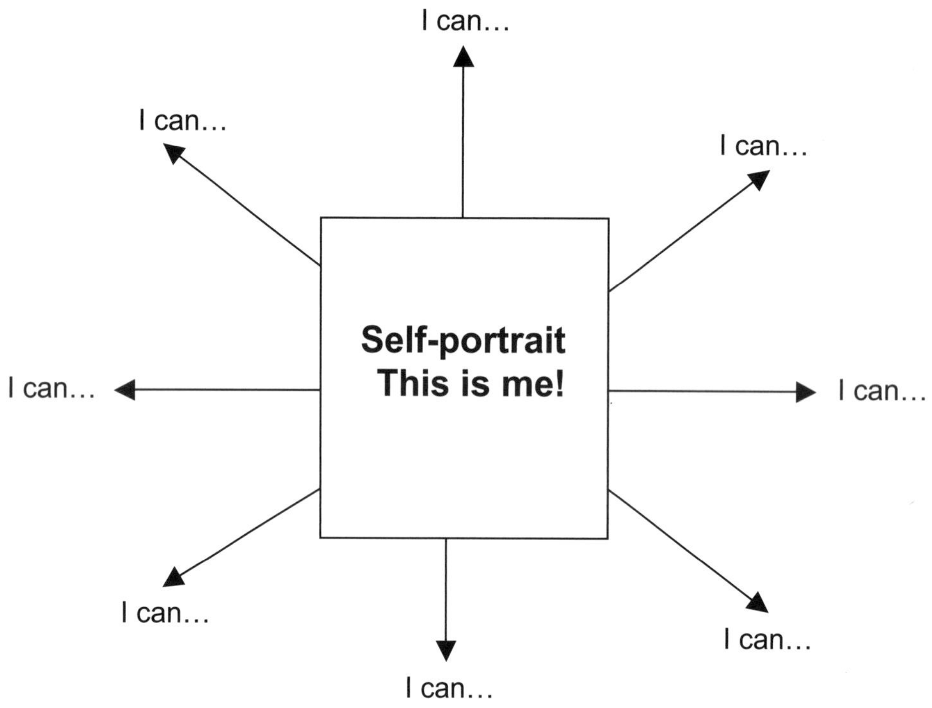

I can…

I can…

I can…

I can…

Self-portrait
This is me!

I can…

I can…

I can…

I can…

The Incredibles

This fun activity helps you to discover the superheroes in your family, class or group!

What you need:

- Paper
- Colouring pens
- Pencils
- Badge blanks that you can decorate yourself

What you do:

- Some of the television science fiction and fantasy series have several superheroes with different skills. In order to solve a problem, or to save the world, they need to use all their different skills and work together as a team.
- Think about each of the people in your family, class or group. What are their special skills? What kind of superhero are they? How do they use their hero-skills to help your family, class or group sort out its everyday challenges and reach its goals?
- Make a list of the superheroes your family, class or group needs to help meet its challenges or reach its goals.
- Then decide who has the special skills to be the different superheroes. For example, who is the super-comforter, super-fixer, super-tidier, super-cheerer-upper, super-brave-person, super-nurse, super-peacemaker, etc.?
- When you've decided which super-skill each person has, work in twos or threes to make superhero badges for each other.

Some things to talk about together:

- What are some of the goals and challenges your family or group faces?
- What superheroes have you already discovered?
- What new superheroes might you need?
- How can all superheroes work together to help your group or family reach your goals or deal with your challenges?
- How can we let each other know when a superhero is needed?

Compliments cards

Send a private compliment using the postcard.

Fold

Fold and seal

Good friends have good listening

How do we feel?

(a) When we are listened to?
(b) When we are not listened to?

Stop, think and reflect:
What non-verbal behaviours would you observe in a GOOD LISTENER?
Use the sub-headings to help prompt your thinking.

1. Voice ....

2. Eye contact ....

3. Spatial distance ....

4. Fiddling movements ....

5. Positive ....

6. Head movements ....

7. Facial expression ....

8. Gestures ....

The habit of using cognitive behaviour therapy (CBT) skills

Information Sheet (1)

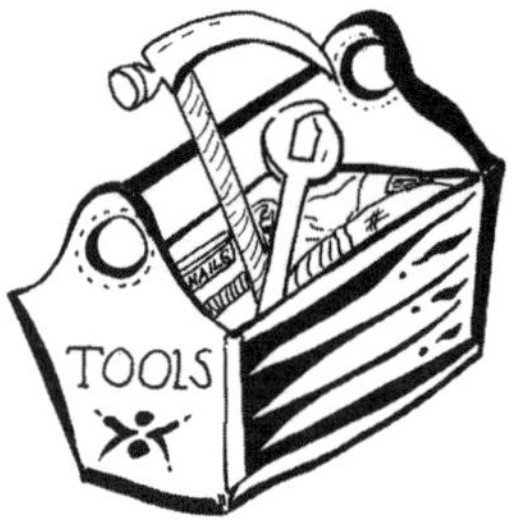

A set of tools to help you deal with
problems and find the best solutions.

Looking at Links ......

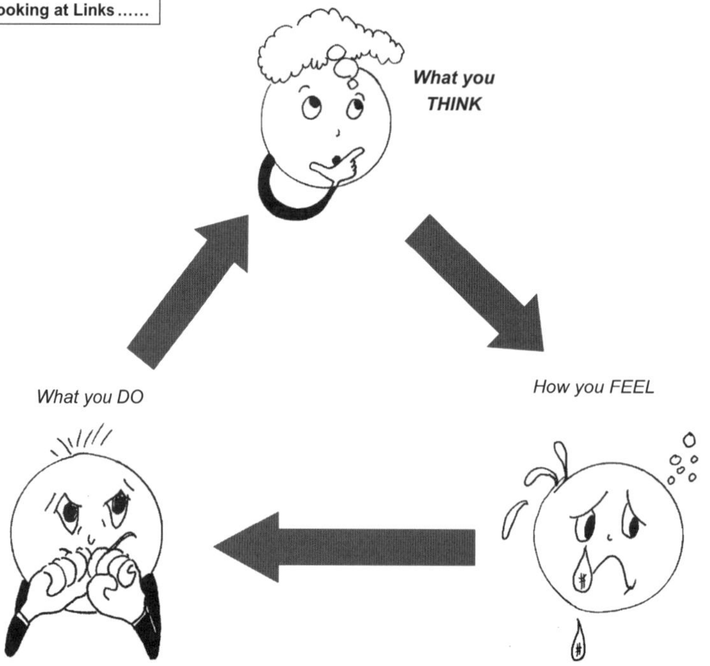

*What you
THINK*

What you DO

How you FEEL

Cognitive behaviour therapy (CBT)

Information sheet (2)

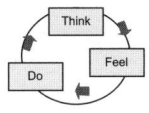 | HOW do the LINKS work? |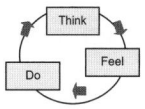

Some examples:

Think... ➡	Feel... ➡	Do... ➡
I'm useless at meeting new people	I feel scared and nervous when I meet new people	I don't talk to them and go quiet
No one in my form likes me	I feel sad and angry	I avoid going out at break and start to bunk off school
I'm rubbish at Maths	I feel dumb and fed up	I stop trying because I know I'll get it all wrong

Statement: how you think about something will become true

STOP, THINK & REFLECT

- Is this true?
- Can we change the way we think?
- Can we handle our problems differently to change how we feel and what we do?
- Can we gain more CONTROL over what happens to us in our lives?

© 2015, *Using Positive Psychology to Enhance Student Achievement*, Tina Rae and Ruth MacConville, Routledge

A good time

Think about your most recent good time.
Write &/Draw:

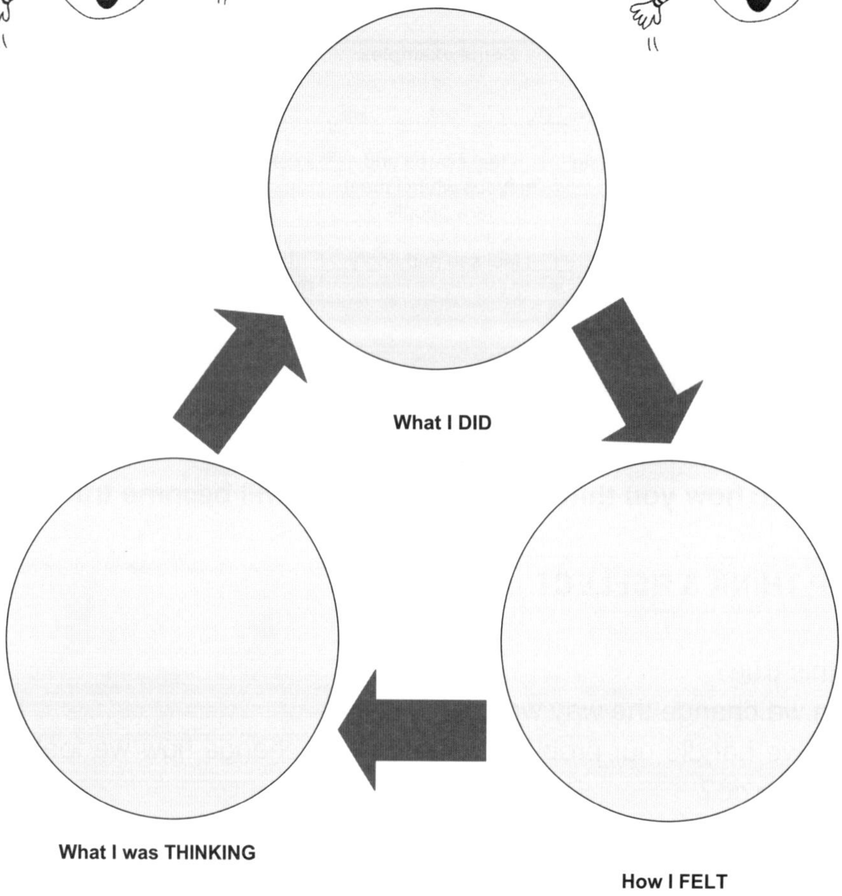

What I DID

How I FELT

What I was THINKING

Think about your most recent good time.

Write &/Draw:

**What I
DID**

**What I was
THINKING**

**How I
FELT**

A bad time!

Think about your most recent bad time.
Write &/Draw:

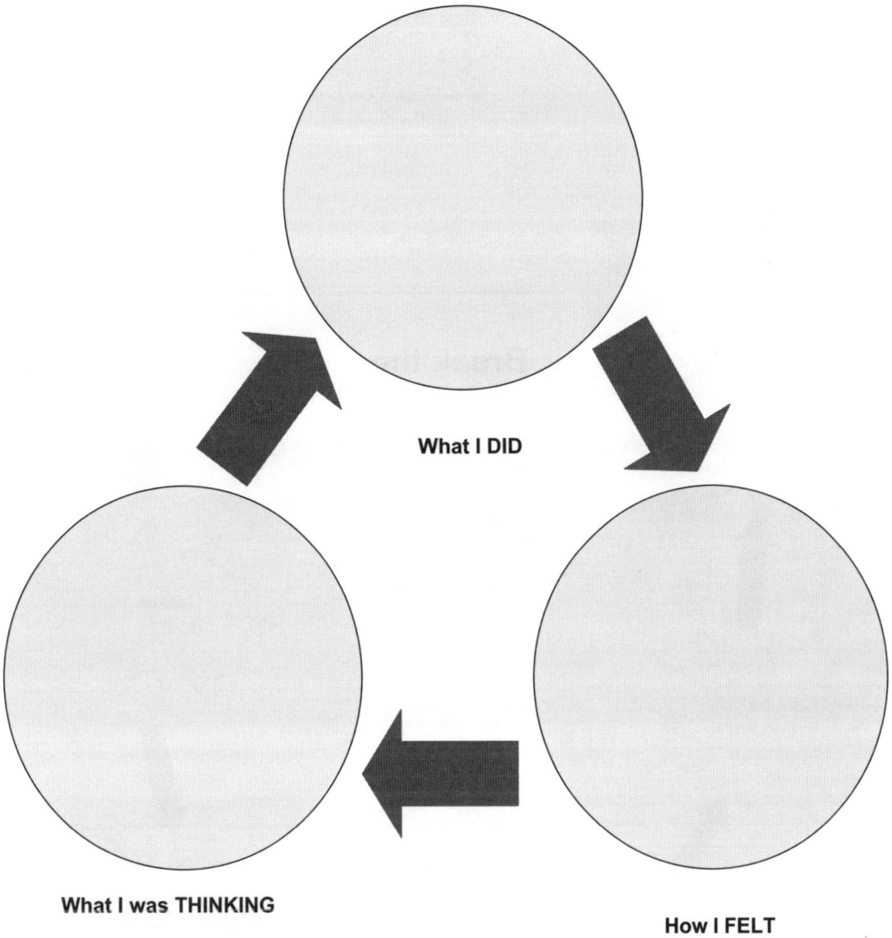

What I DID

What I was THINKING

How I FELT

Are you in a negative trap???

Think about your most recent bad time.

Write / Draw:

**What I
DID**

**What I was
THINKING**

**How I
FELT**

Are you in a negative trap???

A good habit: breaking the negative cycle

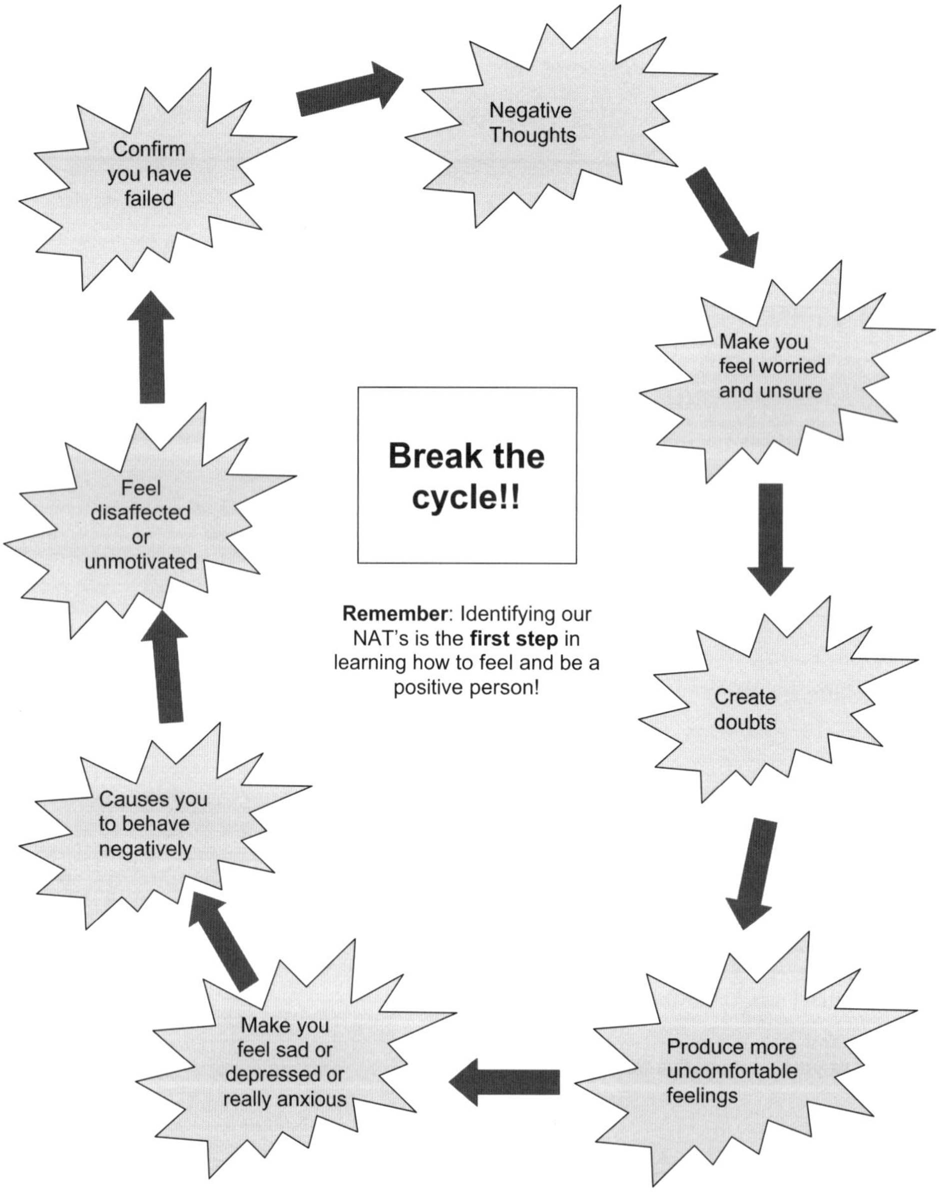

Confirm you have failed

Negative Thoughts

Make you feel worried and unsure

Break the cycle!!

Remember: Identifying our NAT's is the **first step** in learning how to feel and be a positive person!

Create doubts

Feel disaffected or unmotivated

Causes you to behave negatively

Produce more uncomfortable feelings

Make you feel sad or depressed or really anxious

Positives and negatives

\+

\-

Stop, Think & Reflect!

PAT's (Positive Automatic Thoughts)	**NAT's** (Negative Automatic Thoughts)
What positive thoughts do you have:	What negative thoughts to you have:
(A) ABOUT YOU	(B) ABOUT YOU
(C) ABOUT YOUR FUTURE	(D) ABOUT YOUR FUTURE

Faulty thinking

Recognise it and stop it!

There are six kinds of faulty thinking

(1) DOING DOWN!	(2) BLOWING UP!
• Only focus on negatives. • Only see the bad bit in something that was good overall. • Not counting a positive (e.g., 'he only wants to go out with me because he can't find anyone else').	• Making things worse than they are. • It's all or nothing (e.g., I only got 78% and not 100% – it's not good enough!). • Magnifying the problem (e.g., I got the answer wrong and everyone in the class laughed at me! It's a catastrophe! I'll never get over it!).
(3) PREDICTING FAILURE!	**(4) OVEREMOTIONAL THOUGHTS!**
• Mind reading to predict failure (e.g., I bet they are all laughing at me! I know he hates me!) • Fortune-telling – knowing you will fail (e.g., I know I won't be able to do that work/I know they won't like me).	• With this Faulty Thinking our emotions become very strong and cloud the way we think and understand things. • Because we feel bad we presume everything is – the emotions takeover! • We attach negative labels to ourselves (e.g., I'm rubbish, stupid, a loser).
(5) SETTING YOURSELF UP!	**(6) BLAME YOURSELF**
• Setting targets too high and setting ourselves up to fail. • I should, I must, I can't, I want, I shouldn't, etc. • Creating an impossible standard to achieve.	• Everything that goes wrong/is wrong is our fault – even, stuff we have no control over! (e.g., I got into my car and it broke down! I turned on the computer and it crashed!)

How faulty is your thinking?

A self-reflection quiz

Rate yourself on a scale of 0–10 (0 = never, 5 = sometimes, 10 = all the time)

DOING DOWN!

How regularly do you look for the bad/negative things that happen?

| 0 | 1 | 2 | 3 | 4 | 5 | 6 | 7 | 8 | 9 | 10 |

How often do you think things aren't good enough?

| 0 | 1 | 2 | 3 | 4 | 5 | 6 | 7 | 8 | 9 | 10 |

How often do you ignore the good things that happen?

| 0 | 1 | 2 | 3 | 4 | 5 | 6 | 7 | 8 | 9 | 10 |

How regularly do you say the good things weren't 'that good'?

| 0 | 1 | 2 | 3 | 4 | 5 | 6 | 7 | 8 | 9 | 10 |

BLOWING UP!

How often do you turn one negative into a bigger problem?

| 0 | 1 | 2 | 3 | 4 | 5 | 6 | 7 | 8 | 9 | 10 |

How often do you feel that life is just a catastrophe?

| 0 | 1 | 2 | 3 | 4 | 5 | 6 | 7 | 8 | 9 | 10 |

How regularly do you use 'all or nothing' thinking? (e.g., I only got 78% and not 100%. . . . It's not good enough!)

| 0 | 1 | 2 | 3 | 4 | 5 | 6 | 7 | 8 | 9 | 10 |

PREDICTING FAILURE!

How regularly do you think you know what other people are thinking about you?

0   1   2   3   4   5   6   7   8   9   10

How regularly do you say 'I know things will go wrong'?

0   1   2   3   4   5   6   7   8   9   10

OVEREMOTIONAL THOUGHTS!

How often do you think 'I'm a really bad person'?

0   1   2   3   4   5   6   7   8   9   10

How regularly do you think you can never do anything right?

0   1   2   3   4   5   6   7   8   9   10

SETTING YOURSELF UP!

How regularly do you say 'It's not good enough because it's not perfect'?

0   1   2   3   4   5   6   7   8   9   10

How often do you think 'I should do it like that/be like that'?

0   1   2   3   4   5   6   7   8   9   10

How often do you say 'I MUST!'?

0   1   2   3   4   5   6   7   8   9   10

BLAME YOURSELF!

How often do you say 'it's my fault' when things go wrong?

0   1   2   3   4   5   6   7   8   9   10

Information sheet

Controlling thoughts

Facts

- We listen to our thoughts a lot
- We often accept negative thoughts as 'the truth' without really challenging them
- These thoughts can become louder and it becomes harder to hear the positive thoughts
- The more we listen to them, the more uncomfortable and down we fell and the less we do – it's a TRAP!!

The Solution: Distraction

- Helps you take your mind off the negative thoughts
- Helps you take CONTROL of your thoughts by thinking of something else
- You DROWN OUT those negative thoughts by ensuring your mind does what YOU want it to!

Strategies to Try

- Describing what you see
- Puzzle it out!
- Get absorbed
- Self-talking
- Top talk

- Worry box
- Turn it down!
- Test it!
- Bin them!

Test it!

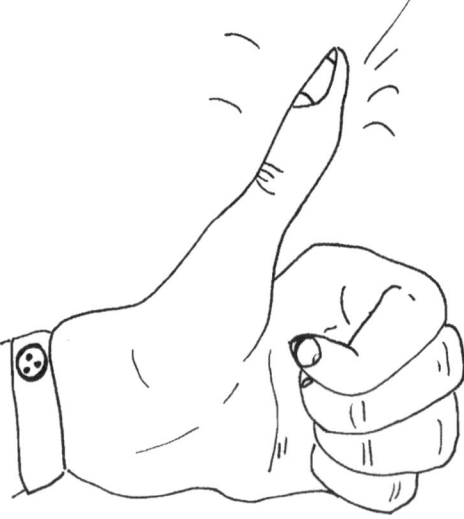

- Identify the negative thought you *most* often have

  _____

- SCALE IT! Out of 10 for how strongly you believe this thought (0 = not strongly; 5 = quite strongly; 10 = extremely strongly)

  $$\frac{}{10}$$

- Design an EXPERIMENT! What test could you set up to see if this is true?
- When will you do this?
- If you think your negative thought is true, what do you think will happen?

  AFTERWARDS . . .

- What actually happened?
- How much/strongly do you now believe this thought?

© 2015, *Using Positive Psychology to Enhance Student Achievement*, Tina Rae and Ruth MacConville, Routledge

Reframing NATs (negative automatic thoughts)

We need to challenge our negative thoughts and always check out the evidence! How true are these thoughts and how can we change negative thoughts into more balanced thoughts? Have a go at reframing these NAT's (the first one is done for you!).

NAT	REFRAME IT!
I can't do that sum!	That sum is difficult, and I might find it hard but I can ask for help.
I always get left out at lunch time!	
I never look as good as everyone else does!	
My work is the worst in the whole school!	
She gave me a bad look because she doesn't like me!	
I'm stupid and thick and useless!	
I won't get picked for the play!	
It's always my fault!	
I'll definitely fail this test!	
He thinks I'm rubbish at everything!	

 **Key questions**

To test your thoughts!

- What is the evidence 'for' this thought?
- What is the evidence 'against' this thought?
- What would my best friend say if they heard my thought?
- What would my teacher say if he/she heard my thought?
- What would my parent/carer say if they heard my thought?
- What would I say to my best friend if he/she had this thought?
- Am I making any thinking mistakes? (e.g., blowing it up, forgetting my strengths or good points, self-blaming or predicting failure/ thinking I know what others are thinking, etc.)

Key Points

GET IT IN PERSPECTIVE!!
We need the evidence – check it out!
Be realistic – life is not problem free!
Challenge and change your thinking to cope more effectively.

A letter of thanks

Studies show that expressing gratitude to others can significantly boost our happiness. It can also have a powerful effect on the recipient and help strengthen your relationship.

Who are you really grateful to?

Think of three people who have been a really positive influence in your life and that you feel really grateful to.

They could be a member of your family, a teacher, a friend, or someone else who has made a real difference in your life.

> Person 1: Who is it and why are you grateful to them?
> Person 2: Who is it and why are you grateful to them?
> Person 3: Who is it and why are you grateful to them?

Now choose one of these people to write to and tell them how grateful you are; perhaps someone you've not thanked properly before.

Think about the impact this person had on you and write a letter to tell them:

- What specifically are you grateful for?
- How did they help you?
- How did it help make the person you are today?

You can write the letter anyway you like – but try to be really in touch with the feeling of being grateful to them as you write.

If possible, arrange to visit the person and read the letter aloud to them. Otherwise post or e-mail the letter to them and maybe follow up with a phone call.

Stop and reflect

> Who did you write your letter of gratitude to? How did it feel?

Message in a bottle

Write a note to a friend to support them in developing their skills and abilities

Tell them about how you developed a talent or ability and overcame problems, developing a skill that you were previously bad at . . .

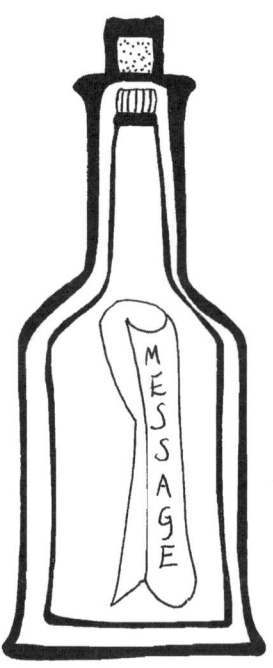

Send the message in a bottle!

Acts of kindness

Doing things to help others is not only good for the recipients – it has a positive payback for our happiness and health, too. When people experience kindness it also makes them kinder as a result – so kindness is contagious!

As the saying goes: 'if you want to feel good, do good'

Perform extra act of kindness each day.

This could be a compliment, a helping hand, a hug, a gift or something else. The act may be large or small and the recipient may not even be aware of it.

Ideally your acts of kindness should be beyond the kind things you already do on a regular basis. And, of course, the acts mustn't put you or others in danger!

Do at least one extra kind act each day for a week, ideally a different one each day.

Here are some ideas for acts of kindness:

1. Give up your seat
2. Hold a door open for someone
3. Give a (sincere) compliment
4. Make someone laugh
5. Give someone a hug
6. Take time to really listen to someone
7. Make someone new feel welcome
8. Let one car In on every journey
9. Give directions to someone who's lost
10. Have a conversation with a stranger
11. Pick up litter as you walk
12. Let someone in front of you in the supermarket queue
13. Tell someone they mean a lot to you
14. Let someone have your parking spot
15. Read a story with a child
16. Offer your change to someone struggling to find the right amount
17. Treat a loved one to breakfast in bed
18. Buy cakes or fruit for your colleagues
19. Invite your neighbour round for a drink and a chat
20. Offer to help with someone's shopping
21. Tell someone if you notice they're doing a good job
22. Pass on a book you've enjoyed
23. Say sorry (you know who to)
24. Forgive someone for what they've done
25. Visit a sick friend, relative or neighbour
26. Buy an unexpected gift for someone

27. Bake something for a neighbour
28. Pay for someone in the queue behind you
29. Do a chore that you don't normally do
30. Help out someone in need
31. Offer to look after a friend's children
32. Offer to mow your neighbour's lawn
33. Donate your old things to charity
34. Give food to a homeless person and take time to talk with them
35. Visit someone who may be lonely
36. Give blood
37. Get back in contact with someone you've lost touch with
38. Organise a fundraising event
39. Volunteer your time for a charity
40. Plan a street party

Tick against each of these acts you have already completed once in your life!

Random acts of kindness diary

Do at least one kind act each day for a week, ideally a different one each day.

Ideally your random act of kindness should be something beyond the kind things you do on a regular basis.

Use this sheet to keep a record of your acts of kindness. You can also note down how you felt about doing them and whether you found them easy or difficult.

1. Day/date:

What did you do? Who for? How did it go?

2. Day/date:

What did you do? Who for? How did it go?

3. Day/date:

What did you do? Who for? How did it go?

4. Day/date:

What did you do? Who for? How did it go?

5. Day/date:

What did you do? Who for? How did it go?

6. Day/date:

What did you do? Who for? How did it go?

7. Day/date:

What did you do? Who for? How did it go?

Introduction

Whilst we are aware that many teachers and facilitators will feel comfortable in using the three-part resource in a flexible way and also see how the resources such as mindfulness activities can be incorporated across the curriculum, others may wish to systematically work through a programme which is structured and presented in a set framework.

We have consequently arranged some of the resources from the three-part resource and supplemented these with some additional ideas and activities to form a 10-part programme for use with children and young people in a range of learning contexts. The sessions introduce the concept of happiness, building happy habits and using such habits to promote overall well-being. There is a real focus here on developing motivation, an outward focus and specifically getting into the habit of using key strategies from cognitive behaviour therapy (CBT) and Mindfulness on a daily basis.

The sessions are relatively easy to follow and have clear instructions for both the students and the facilitators concerning modes of delivery and expectations. There is, of course, room for flexibility here in that additional resources and materials from the three-part resource bank can also be used in conjunction with the resources set out in each session. This may be useful in terms of providing reinforcement opportunities and specifically when seeking to create a sense of mastery of key skills and strategies from CBT and Mindfulness.

Using CBT approaches to build happy habits

Cognitive behaviour therapy (CBT) reveals the role that thoughts play in relation to both our emotions and our behaviours. This approach provides individuals with a way of talking about themselves, their world and people who inhabit it, so that they are more able to understand how what they do effects both their thoughts and feelings, and vice versa.

This approach focuses on the role that thoughts play in regard to both emotions and behaviour, and advocates that change in thought processes can have a significant effect upon altering behaviours. Unlike many of the talking treatments that traditional therapists have used, CBT focuses upon the 'here and now', as well as ways to improve the individual state of mind in the present time. This is innovative in the sense that there is no focus on the causes of distress or past symptoms as there evidently is with traditional psychotherapy.

Restructuring thought processes

Young people are frequently flooded with anxious and negative thoughts and doubts. These messages will often reinforce a state of inadequacy and/or low levels of *self-esteem*. The process of cognitive behaviour therapy helps to support young people in reconsidering these negative assumptions. It also allows them to *learn how* to change their self-perceptions in order to improve their mental and emotional state – this is the key aim of this kind of intervention. Changing negative thought patterns or opinions will ultimately help young people to become more able to control and change their behaviours, but this does take practise. This is why, as with anger management interventions, another key element of the approach is the requirement to learn, and to put into practise, the skills or strategies discussed in any session.

ABC

The CBT approach breaks the problems into smaller parts. This enables the student to see how they're connected and how they affect them. This follows a process of A, B, C as follows:

- **A**, or the **activating event**, is often referred to as the 'trigger' – the thing that causes you to engage in the negative thinking.
- **B** represents these negative **beliefs**, which can include thoughts, rules and demands, and the meanings the individual attaches to both external and internal events.
- **C** is the **consequences**, or emotions, and the behaviours and physical sensations accompanying these different emotions. It is important to highlight and discuss with the students how the way that they think about a problem can affect how they feel physically and emotionally. It can also alter what they do about it. This is why the key aim for CBT is to break the negative, viscous cycle that some students may find themselves in. For example, if you think that you will get your work wrong you feel angry, and then you don't give it a try in case it is wrong.

Core beliefs

Core beliefs are the strong, enduring ideas that we may have about ourselves. This kind of belief system gives rise to rules, demands or assumptions which in turn produce automatic thoughts. Core beliefs generally fall into three main categories: beliefs about yourself; beliefs about other people in the world; beliefs that are either positive or negative. What is important is to identify our core beliefs and to also consider why these may or may not be unhelpful. In this way we can begin to identify negative automatic thoughts (NATs).

What are NATs?

Negative core beliefs can cause us to engage in a number of faulty thinking strategies. Individuals will tend to focus on negative automatic thoughts. Some of these thoughts that students may hold about themselves could include the following:

- I always look ugly.
- I don't understand this work.
- He thinks I'm stupid and an idiot.
- She gave me a nasty look.

- I'm just such a useless person.
- I can't do that and I'll never be able to do it like other people can.

When working with students in identifying such faulty thinking, the main aim is to encourage them to break the negative cycle. These NATs can arise from a number of errors in our thinking, including the following six types of faulty thinking:

1. **Doing ourselves down** – only focusing on the negatives and seeing bad things about ourselves.
2. **Blowing things up or catastrophising** – making things worse than they really are.
3. **Predicting failure** – setting your mind ready to predict failure at all costs.
4. **Overemotional thoughts** – this is when your emotions become extremely powerful and cloud your judgement.
5. **Setting yourself up** – setting yourself targets that are too high so that you know then you will fail.
6. **Blaming yourself** – thinking that everything that goes wrong is your own fault.

When working with young people, it is important to allow them time to consider the effects that these NATs can have prior to them beginning to implement some changes.

Behavioural experiments

One of the most helpful interventions for developing new and more positive belief systems, and for challenging these negative automatic thoughts, is to **test the evidence**. Students can engage in the following questioning process:

- What is the evidence for this thought?
- What is the evidence against this thought?
- What would my best friend say if they heard my thought?
- What would my teacher say if he heard my thought?
- What would my parents or carers say if they heard my thought?
- What would I say to my best friend if s/he had this same thought?
- Am I making mistakes? For example, blowing it up, forgetting my strengths or good points, self-blaming or predicting failure or thinking that I can mind read what others are thinking?

This kind of strategy is particularly useful in terms of reinforcing the need to gather accurate evidence. What we believe about ourselves is not always true. It is not how others always see us and these kinds of beliefs need to be challenged in this way. Using this sort of questioning process, and gathering evidence in the form of such a behavioural experiment, is a particularly positive strategy for beginning to identify and challenge unhelpful beliefs that students may carry.

Further strategies to implement change

Reframing is another useful tool for students to learn and practise. Negative thoughts can be reframed into more positive, balanced and realistic ones. For example, 'I am just fat' could be reframed as 'I need to lose some weight and tone up a bit but my overall shape isn't that bad', or 'I always get the maths work wrong' could be reframed as 'some of these sums are difficult but I know I can do the basics – I just need to work hard and find help in order to improve my skills.'

Distraction is also a useful strategy by which to banish NATs. Students can be encouraged to control their thoughts by thinking of something else. For example:

- They can describe in detail what they see around them in order to feel calmer. They can attempt to name all of their favourite bands.
- They can use self-talk techniques and repeat a positive coping message until the negative automatic thought has gone.
- They can 'bin' the thoughts by writing them down and then screwing them up and putting them into the bin – symbolically eradicating these negative thoughts.
- Students can also keep a positive diary in order to record positive automatic thoughts (PATs) that may occur during the day, and also engage in realistic goal setting which involves practise.

Overall, what is important when students are engaged in learning and developing these skills is for adults to encourage them to set appropriate targets. Young people need to be reminded that we do not move forwards unless we set realistic goals for ourselves. These should be broken down into small, achievable steps and the ultimate goal continually focused upon. Setting targets allows us to visualise where we want to be in the future and if we feel that we have nowhere to go, nor nothing to move towards, then ultimately we will not be able to affect the change necessary.

This 10-session programme uses a range of tools from CBT and pays particular attention to the skills of reframing and recognising negative automatic thoughts. However, it is important to note that this is a mere introduction and like all the strategies introduced here, we would hope that the facilitator would emphasise the need for these to become habits – the kind of healthy and happy habits that children and young people engage in on a daily basis in order to foster and maintain well-being. These habits of positive thinking, reframing, relaxing, being in the flow, mastery, recognising strengths, etc., can become automatic – in a sense, just like the habit of brushing your teeth!

The use of mindfulness

In the same way, it is hoped that the value of mindfulness-based activities will also become apparent and part of the thinking and ultimately, the daily habits and rituals of the students participating in the programme. Mindfulness can initially be introduced as an intervention which focuses on developing attention skills. The students will be asked to pay attention to each and every moment, not to make any judgements about those moments and also to be able to accept themselves for simply being the people that they are. Stopping and being still and thinking and noticing what is going on are body experiences and how we are thinking and responding to those thoughts is something that will help all of us in both the short and longer terms. The facilitator(s) can explain to the students that it is possible to allow themselves to have feelings without allowing those feelings to overcome us. Mindfulness, as introduced in this programme, will ultimately help them to relax more and to remain calm when things go wrong or they begin to get stressed.

The processes will also encourage the young people to show themselves compassion and tolerance and not to constantly compare themselves to other people. It is this kind of behaviour that generally leads us to feel very unhappy with both ourselves and our lives in general. The facilitator(s) can explain to the students that they will engage in activities which will help them learn about themselves and each other. For example, they will undertake activities that will help them become more aware of physical sensations, thoughts and feelings. They will be taught how to slow down, to focus on their breathing and to be able to simply accept a thought, recognise and then let it go without making any judgement about it. They will then be encouraged to make regular times which they allocate to building these skills and habits, consequently experiencing an increase in their confidence in using mindfulness tools and strategies.

The structure of the programme

The 10 sessions in this programme are arranged as follows:

1. Introductory session: Happy Habits
2. Building the strength habit
3. The mindfulness habit
4. Building healthy habits
5. The gratitude habit
6. Boosting positive emotions habit
7. The confidence and flow habits
8. The visualisation and mastery habits
9. Savouring and motivation habits
10. A friendly future habit

Each session (apart from Session 1) will be structured as follows:

- Introduction and Aims
- Icebreaker
- Strategy Sheets/Practise
- Take Home Habit Task
- Plenary and Evaluation

We would suggest that this group intervention would best be delivered by two facilitators and would also consider that reference to the following checklist might also be helpful when embarking upon this course for the first time. It is important that those who are promoting the well-being and development of 'happy habits' in young people feel secure in their own knowledge and understanding of the key concepts and also have some experience of managing group processes.

Facilitator's checklist

Preparation for delivery of this programme must include both practical considerations relating to room use, resources and so on, as well as reflection on your own experience of behaviour change and well-being, your skills as a facilitator and the need to reduce risk and create a learning environment which feels safe for children and young people.

This checklist has been developed to help facilitators prepare thoroughly. It may be useful as an exercise to help you establish priorities for discussion or action. It is not definitive and it may be appropriate to add other points that relate more specifically to your situation or school context.

While it is not essential that you have all the knowledge, skills and experience implied below, it is essential that you are aware of your strengths and weaknesses and that you take the necessary steps to ensure you are well prepared.

Remember, behavioural change is an emotional change is an emotional topic and may arouse strong feelings and reactions. It is important that the facilitator feels able to 'hold' a group and is prepared to deal with difficulties that arise. It is important that the learning process itself is 'emotionally literate' and that a supportive empathic and caring ethos is promoted from the start.

We recommend that two facilitators run this programme. This could be a 'lead facilitator' (e.g., a learning mentor or teacher) supported by a learning support assistant. Having two facilitators means you can withdraw individuals if necessary. It also means one of you can take on an observer role if appropriate.

The lead facilitator should:

- Have experience of/a secure understanding of Positive Psychology and CBT and Mindfulness processes and techniques.
- Have experiencing of delivering group work and Circle Time.
- Have a positive approach and proven skills in relation to social inclusion.
- Be committed to developing their own emotional literacy.
- Have a reflective approach to their teaching and learning.
- Understand how emotional literacy promotes mental health and school achievement.

Before starting this programme, facilitators should discuss any personal experience of behaviour change with each other which may be helpful or unhelpful. Consideration should also be given to ways in which you will support each other during the programme.

Whole-school readiness

- In your opinion, has the school dealt well with mental health issues amongst staff and pupils?

- Does the school have an active policy on behaviour and bullying?
- Does the school have a member of staff responsible for special educational needs (SEN), travellers, homeless, looked after, adopted children and refugees?
- Are school exclusions dealt with systematically, fairly and as a last resort?
- Will you be supported by senior management?
- How will you deal with colleagues or parents/carers who have a strong negative reaction to this work?
- How will you explain the work to parents/carers?
- Is there a whole school policy on emotional literacy and well-being?
- To whom are you accountable in this role?

Reducing risk

- Think about writing a letter to parents and carers to either secure their consent or inform them of your intentions.
- Identify potentially vulnerable children prior to starting the group.

Do you feel confident to manage the contributions of:

- Pupils at risk of exclusion?
- Pupils underachieving?
- What self-management strategies will you use to prepare yourself for each session?
- Can you provide 1:1 time for pupils who need it? How will you identify those pupils?
- Will you evaluate each session on the same day as it is held?
- How will 'lessons learned' when running this group be fed into future planning for this work?
- When planning the programme identify 'what if . . . ?' Worst-case scenarios. This will help you anticipate and prevent problems.
- Who will provide supervision for you? Do you have access to an experienced professional who could talk on this role? How would this support ensure your safety and how will you access and find this support?

Inclusion

- Are the classroom and the curriculum accessible to all learners? Will your sessions include everyone?
- How will you manage the introduction of differentiated tasks for some learners?
- How will you pay attention to different learning styles?
- Will your resources and anecdotes portray the world as exclusively young, white, middle-class, able-bodied and heterosexual?
- Will your displays represent the cultural diversity of our society? Will they challenge stereotypes?

- Will you challenge discriminatory attitudes and practises of some pupils constructively?
- How are the needs of bilingual and ethnic minority learners met?
- What are your own beliefs about behaviour change and the use of therapeutic tools to achieve this?
- What are the dominant cultural values and/or religious beliefs in the school? In what ways will this help or hinder the effective delivery of the programme?

Group work and team-teaching

- Do you understand the difference between group work and working in groups?

Have you and your co-facilitator discussed:

- How much you will disclose
- How and when you will evaluate each session
- What happens if one of you is absent
- What will you do if a pupil is absent
- The benefits of having one of you taking an observer role for some activities
- A draft opening statement for your first session
- Suggested ground rules
- How will you manage any resulting paperwork?
- Do you have any strategies for managing difficult individuals in groups? Do you have a shared view on how you will manage difficulties?
- Discuss how you would like to give each other feed back?

(Adapted from T. Rae and D. Weymont, 2006, *Supporting Young People Coping with Grief, Loss and Death*, London: Paul Chapman Publishing, p. 7–9 [facilitators checklist]).

Session 1

Introductory session: Happy habits

Introduction and aims

In this session the students are introduced to the concept of happiness as an experience common to all human beings in their daily lives. They're encouraged to reflect upon their own levels of happiness and to gain an understanding of 'habits' which promote happiness and overall well-being and the need to develop these in our daily lives. They are also encouraged to develop a series of achievable happiness targets. The aims are as follows:

- To define happiness
- To distinguish between good and bad habits
- To reinforce the fact that happiness can be increased
- To formulate and clarify group rules for the programme
- Students to utilise self-reflection strategies in order to make more real a happier existence.

The facilitator may wish to also provide the students with an outline of the happy habits programme. The main objectives can be reinforced in order to ensure that students fully understand the purpose of this series of skills based sessions. These will be as follows:

- To provide students with a confidential and supportive framework in which they can begin to reflect upon their feelings, behaviours, actions and happiness levels.
- To allow each student in the group to begin to understand the nature and causes of stress and anxiety both in themselves and others.
- To encourage students to distinguish between positive and negative responses to stress and anxiety.
- To encourage an understanding regarding the ways in which happy habits from positive psychology can support the maintenance and further development of well-being.
- To increase students' awareness regarding the fact that people will need different levels of support at different times in their lives.
- To encourage students to further develop empathy for others alongside their own problem-solving skills within a supportive framework.
- To encourage students to consider and practise a range of strategies from CBT and Mindfulness approaches for coping with difficult feelings and events we may all encounter on a daily basis.
- To increase students' level of confidence in their own abilities to cope with stressful situations and conflicts in an assertive and positive way and to be able to bounce back and not give up when the going gets tough.

- To ensure that students are aware of their own strengths and the importance of continually building and using these throughout their lives.
- To understand and use the happy habits of engaging in flow activities, savouring the positives, and the need to develop friendly habits in order to show gratitude and sustain positive relationships over time.

Icebreaker

The facilitator can pose the question 'what is happiness?' The students can then contribute their own ideas and definitions. These can be recorded on a whiteboard or flipchart as appropriate and it may then be useful for the group, as a whole, to formulate their own agreed definition. Students may wish to also focus upon some of the causes of happiness that they are currently experiencing in their lives.

Group rules

The setting up of group rules is essential in terms of ensuring a positive tone and the safety and security of all the students involved in the programme. The students are required to discuss and agree their own group rules so as to ensure ownership and sessions. The rules may well include some of the following:

- We will all try to concentrate and be reflective in each session so that we can all contribute.
- We won't laugh at others or put them down.
- We'll listen to each other's ideas and show respect for them.
- We will take turns to talk.
- We will keep the privacy and confidentiality in this group.
- We will try to cooperate with each other at all times.
- We will choose not to say anything if we don't want to.

The facilitator may also wish to reinforce the fact that there may be things that are not appropriate to discuss within this context. This would include any situation which would appear to be putting an individual student at risk. Should such an issue arise then it will be necessary to ensure that the student has access to one to one time with the facilitator in order to talk through the particular situation or difficulty. Disclosure of any abuse of any kind would obviously need to be dealt with via the usual support system and referral mechanisms within the school.

Strategy sheets

What is happiness?
This activity is designed to build upon the initial thought storm and to engage the students in considering the two main areas of happiness in terms of

feeling good and *flourishing*. The Greek philosopher Aristotle thought that you needed to feel good and to flourish in order to achieve true happiness. The students are asked to identify what they themselves can do in order to increase both aspects in their own lives.

What is a habit?

In this activity the students can be asked to define the nature of a habit and also consider and distinguish between those habits which are bad for us and decrease well-being overall and those that my well help us to maintain and further build our emotional, mental and physical health.

Information sheet

This information sheet asks the students to reflect in even more depth on the notion of happiness and to answer a series of questions. It may well be useful to ask the students to work together in smaller groups in order to share and compare their responses and to then be able to highlight any agreements or differences. The questions are wide ranging and include the following: Does happiness come to us by accident? In what ways can we make ourselves happy (think about those happy habits)? Some people who are seriously ill appear to be happy all the time. How is that possible? Is it better not to think about being happy or unhappy? What are the things in your daily life that constantly make you happy? How could you be happier than you are now? Are these important factors in unhappiness? Being without love, having nothing to do, being ill, being lonely and hurting someone else.

Clearly, there is a great deal of information on this sheet and a significant level of discussion may well be the result. We would therefore suggest that the facilitators may well wish to allocate some additional time to this aspect of the session or alternatively, conduct this as a whole group discussion with the facilitator(s) acting as a scribe and managing the discussion in terms of working through each item with the group as a whole.

10 habits to happier living

The students are here introduced to 10 habits to happier living. In smaller groups, the students can discuss what they understand each of these 'habits' to mean for them in their lives. The questions posed are as follows: How do you think, for example, that you can get into the habit of building your resilience on a daily basis or increasing your levels of self-acceptance and direction? What are the 'habits' you can build into your daily life?

Take home habit task

Happiness log format

This take home habit task requires the students to keep a daily happiness log. They are asked to record their activities and moments when they felt happy or made others happy.

This is not simply intended to increase the feel good factor around noticing the positives but also to reinforce that the happy habit of 'looking for the good' is something that really does work in terms of increasing levels of positivity overall.

Plenary and evaluation

The students can finally focus upon the following series of questions:

- What have we learnt about happiness in this session?
- Have we increased our knowledge?
- Have we gained any further useful strategies or techniques?
- Did everyone feel supported and comfortable?
- What was the most useful?
- What was the least useful?
- How would you change or adapt this session to make it more engaging and useful for other students in the future?

Session 1 Our happy habits group rules

Our group rules for the happy habits course are:

-
-
-
-
-
-

Session 1 Our happy habits group rules

What is happiness?

There are two major ideas of happiness and well-being.

| **Feeling good** | and | **Flourishing** |

Feeling good is about having positive feelings, experiencing pleasure and good relationships.

Flourishing is the result of living a good and meaningful life. You flourish when you feel that you are leading a good life and when others think you are too.

The Greek philosopher Aristotle thought that you needed to feel good and to flourish in order to achieve true happiness.

Things I can do to feel good	Things I can do to flourish
Have fun!	Develop my talents!
Challenge negative thoughts!	Be future focused!
Keep fit!	Set good goals!
Have positive relationships!	Make a positive contribution to others!

What is a habit?

We can have both 'good' and 'bad' habits and these can affect how we live our lives and our overall well-being.

Make a list of habits that you think are good and those you consider to be bad. Discuss with others and see if there is any agreement.

Good habits	Bad habits

Do you think that some of our habits can help us to become happier people? What is a happy habit? What things do you do on a daily basis that make you experience more positive feelings?

Information Sheet

Happiness

We sometimes hear people saying 'My schooldays were the happiest days of my life.' But most young people will know that being at school and being dependent on their family gives them personal problems that sometimes make happiness difficult and people who have left school know that being dependent and responsible in various ways gives them personal problems that make happiness difficult. Who is happy? Let's have a think!

STOP AND REFLECT!

How important are these factors in being happy?

Money	Having power
Being young	Being important or famous
Good health	Interesting work
Good friends	Love
Having a car, a nice house, a fur coat	Having children

Does happiness depend on factors like these? Or does it depends on a person's attitude to life and his attitude to other people?

Does happiness come to us by accident? In what ways can we make ourselves happy? (think about those happy habits) Some people who are seriously ill appear to be happy all the time. How is that possible? Is it better not to think about being happy or unhappy?

What are the things in your daily life that constantly make you happy? How could you be happier than you are now?

Are these important factors in unhappiness?

Being without love

Having nothing to do

Being ill

Being lonely

Hurting someone else

Who is the happiest person you know? Why is he or she happy?

Is it possible to be happy without other people? Would you be happy if you lived alone in a forest or desert? What can a lonely person, for example a widow or a divorced woman do to make her life happy?

Are men and women happy in different ways and for different reasons?

Why do some people have a feeling of guilt when they are very happy? Is it wrong or selfish to be happy?

Is it important to be happy?

Ten 'habits' to happier living

There are 10 'habits' to happier living. The first 5 focus on how we interact with the OUTSIDE world and the second 5 come from WITHIN us! Look at these 10 habits very carefully. . . .

GIVING	Do things for others
RELATING	Connect with people
EXERCISING	Take care of your body
APPRECIATING	Notice the world around
TRYING OUT	Keep learning new things
DIRECTION	Have goals to look forward to
RESILIENCE	Find ways to bounce back
EMOTION	Take a positive approach
ACCEPTANCE	Be comfortable with who you are
MEANING	Be part of something bigger

In smaller groups, discuss what you understand each of these 'habits' to mean for you in your life. How do you think, for example, that you can get into the habit of building your resilience on a daily basis or increasing your levels of self-acceptance and direction? What are the 'habits' you can build into you daily life?

© 2015, *Using Positive Psychology to Enhance Student Achievement*, Tina Rae and Ruth MacConville, Routledge

Take home habit task happiness log format

Keep a daily happiness log. Record your activities and moments when you felt happy or made others happy.

What I did	How I or others felt
7.00 a.m.	
8.00	
9.00	
10.00	
11.00	
12.00 p.m.	
1.00	
2.00	
3.00	
4.00	
5.00	
6.00	
7.00	
8.00	
9.00	
10.00	
11.00	

Session 2

Building the strength habit

Introduction and aims

In this session the students are asked to consider how building and using our strengths can prevent stress from escalating further and empower us to live more productive and less anxiety filled lives. The students are introduced to the concept of character strengths and the importance of recognising and building signature strengths – getting into the habit of strengths building! The aims are as follows:

- To highlight the importance of building character and signature strengths.
- To reinforce the need for students to choose to build these strengths in order to maintain a sense of well-being.
- For students to be able to feel empowered to recognise, celebrate and effectively use their strengths whilst also recognising areas for development here.
- To reinforce the skills of self-reflection, self-awareness and appropriate analysis of information.

At the start of this session, the facilitator can request feedback on the Take Home Habit Task, asking students how useful/otherwise they found this activity.

Icebreaker

The facilitator can encourage the students to debate and discuss the following statement 'Image and looking good is a real strength'. Do they agree with this statement? If so, why? Do they not agree? If not, why not? What would they consider to be 'real' strengths? The students can be encouraged to their own reasons for taking on a particular view and these can be recorded on the flipchart or whiteboard by either the facilitator or a student who is nominated for this task.

Strategy sheets

Building strengths and happiness
In this initial thought storm activity the students are asked to identify their strengths. It will be important to highlight that these are not simply things that they are good at but also aspects of their character which are of real

value and help them to cope with life and the good and bad events that they experience.

Seligman's 24 Character Strengths, Part 1
In this activity the students are introduced to Seligman's 24 character strengths and asked to define each one in turn. It is suggested that they work together in pairs or in smaller groups on this particular activity. The instructions are self-explanatory.

Strengths Sort! Seligman's 24 Character Strengths, Part 2
The students are next asked to identify their greatest or strongest strengths. The worksheet presents each strength in a box which the students can cut out and then place in rank order. It may well be the case that this is not an entirely linear process in that some of the strengths may be equal in their view. For example, they might feel that they show equal amounts of humour and gratitude in their lives.

Seligman's 24 Character Strengths, Part 3: My 5 Lowest Strengths
The students next identify their weakest strengths and consider how they might further build upon these in the future.

Take home habit task

Thinking About Skills and Strengths Now and In the Future
The take home habit task asks the students to again reflect upon their strengths and to begin to consider how they might use these in the future. This does not necessarily need to primarily focus upon a chosen career path but can also include the kinds of strengths they might use in their relationships with others in the social context.

Plenary and evaluation

The students can finally focus upon the following series of questions:

- What have we learnt about happiness in this session?
- Have we increased our knowledge?
- Have we gained any further useful strategies or techniques?
- Did everyone feel supported and comfortable?
- What was the most useful?
- What was the least useful?
- How would you change or adapt this session to make it more engaging and useful for other students in the future?

A strength is a positive character trait that feels authentic and energising (Linley 2008)

Building strengths and happiness

Strengths thought-storm!

What are my strengths??

A strength is a positive character trait that feels authentic and energising (Linley 2008)

Seligman's 24 character strengths

Part 1

Define the strengths! Use a dictionary/Google/work with a partner and then feedback to the group.

1. Creativity	13. Citizenship
2. Curiosity	14. Fairness
3. Open-mindedness	15. Leadership
4. Love of learning	16. Forgiveness
5. Keeping perspective	17. Humility
6. Bravery	18. Prudence
7. Persistence	19. Self-regulation
8. Integrity	20. Appreciation of beauty
9. Vitality	21. Gratitude
10. Love	22. Hope
11. Kindness	23. Humour
12. Social intelligence	24. Spirituality

Strengths Sort!
Seligman's 24 character strengths

Part 2

Cut out and rank order which are your greatest strengths?

Creativity	Citizenship
Curiosity	Fairness
Open-mindedness	Leadership
Love of learning	Forgiveness
Keeping perspective	Humility
Bravery	Prudence
Persistence	Self-regulation
Integrity	Appreciation of beauty
Vitality	Gratitude
Love	Hope
Kindness	Humour
Social intelligence	Spirituality

Seligman's 24 character strengths

Part 3
My 5 lowest strengths

Strength	Things I can do to build this
1.	
2.	
3.	
4.	
5.	

Thinking about skills and strengths now and in the future

Things I am good at. . . .	Things I might be able to do with this skill in the future. . . .
*	*
*	*
*	*
*	*
*	*
*	*
*	*
*	*
*	*
*	*
*	*

Session 3

The mindfulness habit

Introduction and aims

In this session the students are asked to consider how using and practising the tools and strategies of mindfulness can prevent stress from escalating further and empower us to live more productive and less anxiety-filled lives. The students are introduced to the concept of mindfulness as a therapeutic intervention emanating from meditation based practises and the importance of recognising how and when these can be helpfully employed – getting into the mindful habit! The aims are as follows:

- To highlight the importance of using meditation based strategies to alleviate stress, tension and anxiety
- To reinforce the need for students to choose to build these strengths in order to maintain a sense of well-being
- For students to be able to feel empowered to recognise, celebrate and effectively use these strategies whilst also recognising areas for development here
- To reinforce the skills of self-reflection, self-awareness and appropriate analysis of information.

At the start of this session, the facilitator can request feedback on the Take Home Habit Task, asking students how useful/otherwise they found this activity.

It may also be helpful to outline some of the benefits of mindfulness for children and young people when initially presenting the first information sheet highlighting the fact that Mindfulness with young people and children will hopefully ensure the following:

- They can balance their emotions and lower stress and anger
- They can practise staying calm and focused on learning in the classroom and therefore further develop their skills in both areas
- They can increase their level of trust that they have between themselves and the adults that look after them, and thus make communication easier overall
- They can develop emotional and cognitive understanding and interpersonal awareness and skills
- They can also be taught how to pay attention; we often say 'pay attention' to children but we don't actually teach them how to do this
- They can also become less reactive and more compassionate to others.

Clearly these are all laudable aims and outcomes, and ones which we would propose for all young people. Ultimately, we want them to be able to achieve the following:

- Better able to focus and concentrate
- Experience increased levels of calm
- Experience decreased levels of stress and anxiety
- Display improved impulse control
- Display increased self-awareness
- Develop natural conflict resolution skills
- Develop more empathy and compassion for others
- Develop and maintain skilful ways to manage difficult emotions.

In essence, we want them to use the mindfulness habit in order to become more able to work, learn and play effectively and productively and to engage meaningfully and positively in their relationships.

Icebreaker

In this activity the facilitator can provide each student with a partner. They are then asked to deduce each other by initially discussing and identifying three things that they would change about themselves or their lives and three things that they would keep the same. The idea here is for students to listen to each others' responses and then to feedback for each other to the rest of the group. For example, this is Gemma; and Gemma has three things that she would change about herself. These are as follows; . . . this is Peter and Peter has three things that he'd like to keep the same about his life and these are as follows . . . etc.

Strategy sheets

The mindfulness habit information sheet

This first sheet introduces the students to the concept and practise of mindfulness. Clearly, within this one session they will not be able to fully appreciate the benefits or gain the expertise of a genuine mindfulness practitioner but it is hoped that they will investigate more fully as a result of this session and the initial activities presented here. It is also important for the facilitator(s) to be aware of the evidence base for this kind of intervention and to also be willing to undertake the learning journey in order to develop their own skills. Mindfulness is a way of paying attention to the present moment. When we're mindful, we become more aware of our thoughts and feelings and better able to manage them.

Being mindful can boost our concentration, improve our relationships and help with stress or depression. It can even have a positive effect on physical problems like chronic pain. Anyone can learn to be mindful. It's simple, you can do it anywhere, and the results can be life-changing. This is the reason why it is included within this programme and resource. We firmly believe that the mindfulness habit can and does promote well-being for those who use it wisely and well.

The raisin exercise

This exercise is a traditional one for introducing the concept of mindfulness and also one that is easy to administer. What is important at the outset is for the students to be seated comfortably in a quiet and peaceful environment.

The facilitator should read the script to the students in a calm and quiet voice, taking time to ensure that each instruction is followed by every individual in the group as follows: Take one of the raisins and hold it in your hand. Look at it carefully, as if you are going to describe it to some being from another planet who has never seen one before. As best you can, be aware of thoughts or images that may sneak in as you look at this object. Simply note that they are just thoughts and return your attention to this object. Notice the colours of the object. What does the surface look like? Is it bumpy or smooth? Explore the object with your eyes and fingers. Is it dry or moist? Notice how the light shines on the object. Bring the raisin to your nose. Does it have any smells? Explore with your eyes, your fingers, and your nose. Is your attention on this raisin in your hand? Then, whenever you're ready, place the raisin in your mouth. Explore the object. Do you notice your mouth watering? As best you can, keep your attention on the raisin and also watch your thoughts. Are the thoughts looking forward to swallowing the raisin and eating another or are they attending to the sensations of the one that is in your mouth? Gently bite the raisin. Taste the flavour. Slowly chew the raisin while noting every sensation. As you swallow the raisin, first note the intention to swallow it. Then feel it slide down your throat and into your tummy. Can you feel that your body is now exactly one raisin heavier than it was a few minutes ago?

The facilitator can then ask the students for feedback – what did they notice? How did this feel? Were they more aware of sensations? Have they ever been so aware of eating something?

A mindful breathing activity

Again, the facilitator can read through the script as the students follow the instructions for mindful breathing as follows: Sit still in a tall position

Get comfortable and then close your eyes

Let the tension float away from your fingers, toes and head

Look closely at one spot on the floor

Notice each breath as it goes in and feel that you are solid and strong

Imagine you're calmer with each breath as you watch the water travel down your mountain

Then stop and reflect and feel how calm you are

Again, it will be useful to ask for feedback – how calming did they find this process? When might they make use of such a habit?

A mindful observation activity

The script can again be read out to the students as follows:

Sit quietly and imagine you are on the top of a big hill. Look down and see the train track picture of a train moving past. As you see each carriage go past, think of it as being one of your thoughts. If you get caught up in your thought and feel as if you've jumped onto the carriage, gently get back up to the top of the hill. Let that thought 'go' – notice it but don't get on the carriage.

Students can then feedback on the experience of mindful observation and try to think about times in their lives when such a strategy may be useful.

Take home habit task

More mindful breathing and Mindfulness record

The final activity to take home is self-explanatory and reinforces the previous breathing one. The students can finally be encouraged to get into the habit of being mindful and to practise skills on a daily basis, recording on the format provided how useful or otherwise they find each of these strategies.

Plenary and evaluation

The students can finally focus upon the following series of questions:

- What have we learnt about happiness in this session?
- Have we increased our knowledge?
- Have we gained any further useful strategies or techniques?
- Did everyone feel supported and comfortable?
- What was the most useful?
- What was the least useful?
- How would you change or adapt this session to make it more engaging and useful for other students in the future?

The mindfulness habit

Introduction

Mindfulness is a way of paying attention to the present moment. When we're mindful we become more aware of our thoughts and feelings and better able to manage them.

Being mindful can boost our concentration, improve our relationships and help with stress or depression. It can even have a positive effect on physical problems like chronic pain.

Anyone can learn to be mindful. It's simple, you can do it anywhere, and the results can be life-changing.

Take 10 minutes each day to do a simple mindfulness meditation

Many of us spend much of our time focused either on the past or on the future, paying very little attention to what is happening right now.

Being mindful involves saying in the moment, spending more time noticing what's going on both inside ourselves and in our surroundings. Rather than trying to change things it involves accepting the way that things are, for better or for worse.

You can follow a free 10-day daily guided meditation on the Headspace website: www.getsomeheadspace.com

You can also download the free Headspace app here:

http://www.getsomeheadspace.com/shop/headspace-meditation-app.aspx

The raisin exercise

Take one of the raisins and hold it in your hand. Look at it carefully, as if you are going to describe it to some being from another planet who has never seen one before. As best you can, be aware of thoughts or images that may sneak in as you look at this object. Simply note that they are just thoughts and return your attention to this object. Notice the colours of the object. What does the surface look like? Is it bumpy or smooth? Explore the object with your eyes and fingers. Is it dry or moist? Notice how the light shines on the object. Bring the raisin to your nose. Does it have any smells? Explore with your eyes, your fingers, and your nose. Is your attention on this raisin in your hand? Then, whenever you're ready, place the raisin in your mouth. Explore the object. Do you notice your mouth watering? As best you can, keep your attention on the raisin and also watch your thoughts. Are the thoughts looking forward to swallowing the raisin and eating another or are they attending to the sensations of the one that is in your mouth? Gently bite the raisin. Taste the flavour. Slowly chew the raisin while noting every sensation. As you swallow the raisin, first note the intention to swallow it. Then feel it slide down your throat and into your tummy. Can you feel that your body is now exactly one raisin heavier than it was a few minutes ago?

Adapted from Semple and Lee (2008, pp. 78–79)

A mindful breathing activity

Breathing out the tension on your mountain

Sit still in a tall position
Get comfortable and then close your eyes
Let the tension float away from your fingers, toes and head
Look closely at one spot on the floor
Notice each breath as it goes in and feel that you are solid and strong
Imagine you're calmer with each breath as you watch the water travel
    down your mountain
Then stop and reflect and feel how calm you are

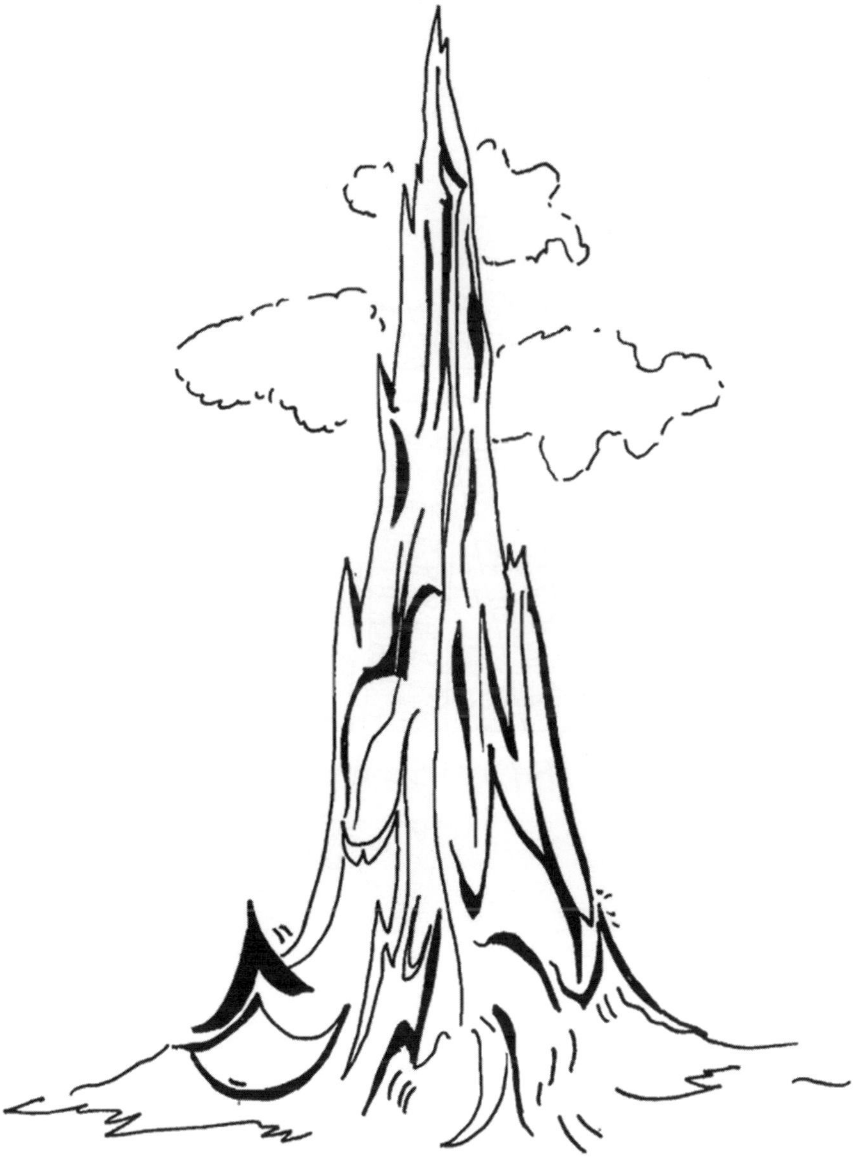

A mindful observation activity

Observe your thoughts to reduce stress

Sit quietly and imagine you are on the top of a big hill. Look down and see the train track picture of a train moving past. As you see each carriage go past, think of it as being one of your thoughts. If you get caught up in your thought and feel as if you've jumped onto the carriage, gently get back up to the top of the hill. Let that thought 'go' – notice it but don't get on the carriage.

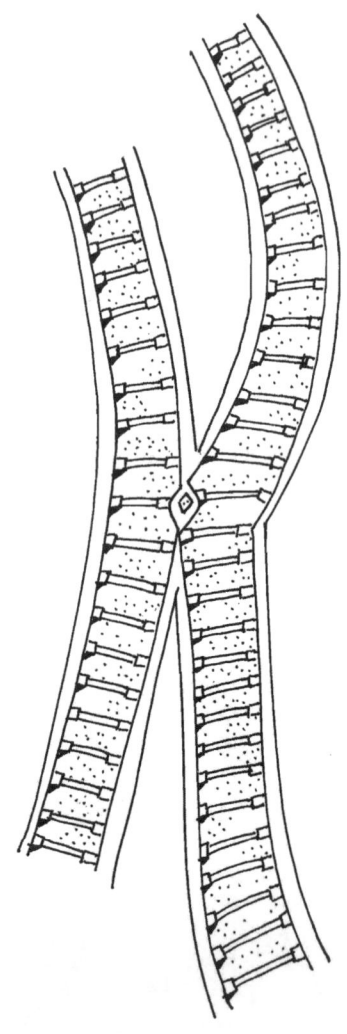

Take home habit task more mindful breathing

Find a comfortable place to sit, with your eyes closed and your spine as straight as you can make it.

Then focus your attention on your breathing. Be very aware of each breath as it goes in and out of your body.

When a thought, or emotion pops into your head accept them, but allow them to float on by (imagine you are pinning them to a cloud or onto a leaf floating down the river).

Focus your attention on the rise and fall of your chest, the feeling of the air entering and leaving your body.

This is mindful breathing!
Practise it!

Mindfulness record

Please try to practise the mindful activities introduced in this session as often as you can. For example, spending a few minutes each day practising breathing exercises will help them to become part of your normal everyday routine! A mindful habit!

Note down in the chart what activity you tried, when you tried it and how it felt, what thoughts or feelings you had and perhaps you could also give it a score out of 5.

You can try these activities at both home and school and then feedback to the group in the next session.

Mindfulness record

When/Date	Where	Activity	Thoughts/ Feelings	Score

Session 4

Building healthy habits

Introduction and aims

In this session the students are asked to consider how using and practising a series of healthy habits can prevent stress from escalating further and empower us to live more productive and less anxiety filled lives. The students are introduced to the concept of healthy options both in terms of protecting physical and mental/emotional health and well-being and the importance of recognising how and when these can be helpfully employed – getting into the healthy habit! The aims are as follows:

- To highlight the importance of using healthy living–based strategies to alleviate stress, tension and anxiety
- To reinforce the need for students to choose to build these strengths in order to maintain a sense of well-being
- For students to be able to feel empowered to recognise, celebrate and effectively use these strategies whilst also recognising areas for development here
- To reinforce the skills of self-reflection, self-awareness and appropriate analysis of information

At the start of this session, the facilitator can request feedback on the Take Home Habit Task, asking students how useful/otherwise they found this activity.

Icebreaker

In this activity the students can be presented with a piece of card on which they are required to record a healthy lifestyle choice. These might include: taking exercise; eating a healthy and well-balanced diet; staying positive; keeping a balance between work, relaxation and managing time effectively; having good friends and relationships; managing money effectively, etc. They can then be prompted to move around the room and record the names of all the students in the group who would choose this option both now and in the future.

Strategy sheets

Getting the healthy habit – which is healthy?
In this activity the students are asked to Tick against the things that they like to do. Then they can talk this through with the rest of the group and consider

the following question: How healthy are your behaviours? Are they really engaging in healthy habits or are there some behaviours that they may need to consider changing or reducing in order to maintain well-being?

Get the keep healthy habit – healthy options
This activity requires the students to cut out a series of statements and to then sort them into order in terms of the most healthy options and least healthy options. This will hopefully generate some debate.

Understand that stress! True or false?
In this activity the students are required to consider how much they really know about stress. The following instructions are given in what is a relatively straight forward activity: What do we know about stress? Is it true or false? Can we agree? Work through the following STRESS FACTS and colour code each statement. The code is as follows: Red = false, green = true

Plan and prioritise to reduce stress
Plan your day and manage your time – provides the students with a format for doing just that. The idea here is to emphasise this as being a truly healthy habit in that it helps to reduce stress and enable us to complete tasks as we need to in order to meet deadlines and maintain overall well-being.

Take home habit task

Leisure pursuits – developing healthy habits and options!
The idea here is to engage the students in keeping a record of leisure activities and to then consider if these provide them with a healthy enough balance between self-indulgence and self-improvement.

Plenary and evaluation

The students can finally focus upon the following series of questions:

- What have we learnt about happiness in this session?
- Have we increased our knowledge?
- Have we gained any further useful strategies or techniques?
- Did everyone feel supported and comfortable?
- What was the most useful?
- What was the least useful?
- How would you change or adapt this session to make it more engaging and useful for other students in the future?

Getting the healthy habit – which is healthy?

Tick against the things you like to do. Then talk it through with the rest of your class. How healthy are your behaviours?

Eat an apple ✓ ✗ ☐ ☐	Play the computer/ go on line ✓ ✗ ☐ ☐	Eat a packet of crisps ✓ ✗ ☐ ☐
Play football ✓ ✗ ☐ ☐	Run/go to the gym ✓ ✗ ☐ ☐	Watch TV ✓ ✗ ☐ ☐
Eat vegetables ✓ ✗ ☐ ☐	Reframe negative thoughts ✓ ✗ ☐ ☐	Use self-calming strategies ✓ ✗ ☐ ☐
Spend time with people who love you ✓ ✗ ☐ ☐	Read a book ✓ ✗ ☐ ☐	Think positive and keep trying ✓ ✗ ☐ ☐
Have a bath/shower ✓ ✗ ☐ ☐	Clean your teeth ✓ ✗ ☐ ☐	Have a fizzy drink ✓ ✗ ☐ ☐

Get the keep healthy habit

Healthy options

Cut out these statements and then sort them into order in terms of the most healthy options and least healthy options.

Taking regular exercise	Not eating junk food
Going to lots of parties	Unprotected sex
Sleeping for 7-9 hours a night	Feeling happy
Low self-esteem	Feeling confident
Eating a 'proper' breakfast	Enjoying hobbies
Eating fruit and vegetables	Having lots of money
Not smoking or taking drugs	Liking other people
Eating a high fat diet	Being optimistic
Not eating sweets or too much sugar	Eating at regular times
Having good friends	Going on holiday
Eating fibre each day	Being able to relax
A low fat diet	A high fat diet
Being the 'right' weight for your height	Not getting anxious about things

Compare your sequence with a friend. Do you agree on what constitutes a healthy life-style? Can you justify your ideas?

Understand that stress! True or false?

What do we know about stress? Is it true or false?

Can we agree? Work through the following STRESS FACTS and colour code each statement. Red = false, green = true

Stress is different for each individual.	Being unfit causes more stress and doing exercise can help you cope better.
Not keeping a balance between work and play can cause stress.	Talking and sharing your feelings can help to solve stress related problems.
Learning to relax can help to reduce stress.	Death or loss causes everyone involved stress.
Family fights or rows cause stress.	Exams cause stress but being organised and planning ahead can reduce this.
Being bullied is a stressor for most students in school.	Too much work causes stress.
Not having enough money makes your stressed.	People can get physical symptoms when they get stressed.
Stress is when you can't cope and feel insecure or helpless.	Solving problems by using step-by-step plans can help reduce stress.
Being organised is a good stress management strategy.	Acting aggressively can increase stress and make stressful situations worse.
Being healthy can reduce stress.	Some stress can be managed whilst other stress can be eliminated.

© 2015, *Using Positive Psychology to Enhance Student Achievement*, Tina Rae and Ruth MacConville, Routledge

Plan and prioritise to reduce stress

Plan your day and manage your time.

List the things you want to achieve tomorrow	My day's plan
1.	7.00 a.m.
	8.00 a.m.
2.	9.00 a.m.
	10.00 a.m.
3.	11.00 a.m.
	12.00 p.m.
4.	1.00 p.m.
	2.00 p.m.
5.	3.00 p.m.
	4.00 p.m.
6.	5.00 p.m.
	6.00 p.m.
7.	7.00 p.m.
	8.00 p.m.
8.	9.00 p.m.
	10.00 p.m.
9.	11.00 p.m.
	midnight
10.	

Can you design your own system or means of prioritising? Have a go. Try it out and feedback to the rest of the group.

Take home habit task leisure pursuits – developing healthy habits and options!

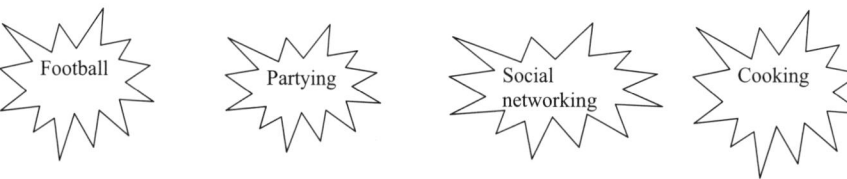

Football   Partying   Social networking   Cooking

Record your leisure pursuits on the chart below.

Then rank order each one – placing the most important one first and the least important last. Then identify the most and least healthy pursuits and consider how you might make your leisure time more productive and enjoyable.

Leisure Activity	Rank Order?	Healthy/Not?

COMPARE your responses with a friend and highlight any similarities and differences.

Session 5

The gratitude habit

Introduction and aims

In this session the students are asked to consider how using and practising a series of gratitude habits which can reinforce the feelings of positivity and overall well-being by ensuring that we feel connected to others. The focus is away from the self and outward facing and this enables us to build a secure base from which to further develop and maintain positive relationships in the social context. Again, such a focus can also empower us to live more productive and less anxiety filled lives. The students are introduced to the concept of gratitude in terms of its importance for maintaining mental/emotional health and well-being and the importance of recognising how and when acts of gratitude can be helpfully employed – getting into the gratitude habit! The aims are as follows:

- To highlight the importance of gratitude to promote a sense of purpose, meaning and overall well-being
- To reinforce the need for students to choose to build these strengths in order to maintain a sense of well-being
- For students to be able to feel empowered to recognise, celebrate and effectively use these strategies whilst also recognising areas for development here
- To reinforce the skills of self-reflection, self-awareness and appropriate analysis of information

At the start of this session, the facilitator can request feedback on the Take Home Habit Task, asking students how useful/otherwise they found this activity.

Icebreaker

In this activity the students are provided with a series of sticky labels (one for each member of the group). They are then required to write down a positive comment for each student in the group on one of these labels. They can then move around the room placing the appropriate label on each individual student. Students can then take it in turns to remove these labels from their jumpers or shirts and place these onto large sheets of paper. This should then result in each individual having a positive scroll as the statements will all be positive and complimentary in nature. The idea here is to reinforce and further build up self-esteem and also highlight the importance of providing positive feedback to each other on a regular basis.

This is a happy habit that we could all engage in on a regular basis to support our own well- being and that of members of our peer group.

Strategy sheets

Three good things: Be grateful!!

Being grateful is about much more than just saying thank you – it's about not taking things for granted and having a sense of appreciation and thankfulness for life.

People who are grateful tend to be happier, healthier and more fulfilled. Being grateful can help people cope with stress and can even have a beneficial effect on heart rate. The students are asked to follow the instructions on the activity sheet: each day write down three good things that happened. They can be anything you feel good about or grateful for.

This is the kind of happy habit that can reinforce feelings of positivity and overall well-being.

And the credits go to . . . : My credit list

This again reinforces why we should be grateful to certain individuals in our lives and the importance of appreciating the kind acts of others who have our well-being at heart. The students are asked to follow these instructions: think of all the people who have helped and supported you. Write a list of credits, identifying what they did to help you.

It may also be a good idea for students to share some of these thoughts and recollections within the group. Again, this can serve to reinforce the importance of recognising and appreciating others.

Compliments cards

The students are asked to send a private compliment using the postcard provided. Alternatively, the facilitator(s) may wish to use 'real' blank postcards which can then be posted – finances allowing!

Take home habit task

A letter of thanks

Studies show that expressing gratitude to others can significantly boost our happiness. It can also have a powerful effect on the recipient and help strengthen your relationship.

The students are asked to write such a letter using the advice and structure provided on the hand out they are initially asked to identify the key people as follows: Who are you really grateful to? Think of three people who have been a really positive influence in your life and that you feel really grateful to. They could be a member of your family, a teacher, a close friend, or someone else who has made a real difference in your life. Now choose one of these people to write to and tell them how grateful you are; perhaps someone you've not thanked properly before.

They are asked to think about the impact this person had on them and to then write a letter to tell them:

- What specifically are you grateful for?
- How did they help you?
- How did it help make the person you are today?

They can write the letter anyway they like – but should try to be really in touch with the feeling of being grateful to them as they write. If possible, they can then arrange to visit the person and read the letter aloud to them. Otherwise they can post or e-mail the letter to them and maybe follow up with a phone call if they feel that this would be appropriate for them and those on the receiving end of this act of gratitude.

Plenary and evaluation

The students can finally focus upon the following series of questions:

- What have we learnt about happiness in this session?
- Have we increased our knowledge?
- Have we gained any further useful strategies or techniques?
- Did everyone feel supported and comfortable?
- What was the most useful?
- What was the least useful?
- How would you change or adapt this session to make it more engaging and useful for other students in the future?

Three good things

Be grateful!!

Being grateful is about much more than just saying thank you – it's about not taking things for granted and having a sense of appreciation and thankfulness for life.

People who are grateful tend to be happier, healthier and more fulfilled. Being grateful can help people cope with stress and can even have a beneficial effect on heart rate.

Each day write down three good things that happened. They can be anything you feel good about or grateful for.

Even on a bad day there are normally some things that we can feel good about. Taking time to be grateful is not about ignoring the bad things – it just helps us focus our attention more on the positive, rather than dwell on the negative.

To get used to the idea, start by filling in the boxes below to describe three good things that happened to you **yesterday** and why they were good.

Try to include **why** you felt each of the things was really good.

Good Thing 1

Example: Best night's sleep for ages so felt much more energetic!

Good Thing 2

Example: Party with Steve and Jane – great to see good friends again.

Good Thing 3

Example: Home in time to talk to Mum. We really had fun together.

Now repeat this activity **at the end of each day** for a week. Use the blank boxes on the following pages to write down your Three Good Things down each day.

And the credits go to . . .

My credit list

Think of all the people who have helped and supported you. Write a list of credits, identifying what they did to help you.

Name	What they did to support/help me

Write notes of thanks to one or all of these people! Show them your gratitude for their kindness.

Compliments cards

Send a private compliment using the postcard.

Fold

Fold and seal

Take home habit task – a letter of thanks

Studies show that expressing gratitude to others can significantly boost our happiness. It can also have a powerful effect on the recipient and help strengthen your relationship.

Who are you really grateful to?

Think of three people who have been a really positive influence in your life and that you feel really grateful to.

They could be a member of your family, a teacher, a close friend, or someone else who has made a real difference in your life.

Person 1: Who is it and why are you grateful to them?
Person 2: Who is it and why are you grateful to them?
Person 3: Who is it and why are you grateful to them?

Now choose one of these people to write to and tell them how grateful you are; perhaps someone you've not thanked properly before.

Think about the impact this person had on you and write a letter to tell them:

- What specifically are you grateful for?
- How did they help you?
- How did it help make the person you are today?

You can write the letter anyway you like – but try to be really in touch with the feeling of being grateful to them as you write.

If possible, arrange to visit the person and read the letter aloud to them. Otherwise post or e-mail the letter to them and maybe follow up with a phone call.

Stop and Reflect

Who did you write your letter of gratitude to? How did it feel?

Session 6

The boosting positive emotions habit

Introduction and aims

In this session the students are asked to consider how using and practising a series of positive thinking habits which can reinforce the feelings of positivity and overall well-being by ensuring that we reduce the extent to which we engage in negative thinking. The focus is in using the key tools and strategies from cognitive behaviour therapy (CBT), recognising the link between our thoughts, feelings and behaviours in order to then pre-empt and reduce the level of negative automatic thinking that we may engage in on a daily basis. Again, such a focus can also empower us to live more productive and less anxiety filled lives. The students are introduced to the concepts of reframing and effective thinking in terms of their importance for maintaining mental/emotional health and well-being and the importance of recognising how and when these strategies can be helpfully employed – getting into the positive thinking habit! The aims are as follows:

- To highlight the importance of positive thinking to promote a sense of purpose, meaning and overall well-being
- To reinforce the need for students to choose to build these strengths in order to maintain a sense of well-being
- For students to be able to feel empowered to recognise, celebrate and effectively use these strategies whilst also recognising areas for development here
- To reinforce the skills of self-reflection, self-awareness and appropriate analysis of information.

At the start of this session, the facilitator can request feedback on the Take Home Habit Task, asking students how useful/otherwise they found this activity.

Icebreaker

The facilitator can pose the question to the students 'what causes negative emotions such as stress in families?' The students can provide their ideas which can be recorded on a flipchart/whiteboard as available and appropriate. Stresses may include the following: jealousy, rivalry, lack of money, loss of job, lack of space, noisy neighbours, issues of control and obedience, insecurities and anxieties, sibling rivalry, etc. The students can then focus upon the following question: what causes happiness within the family context?

Strategy sheets

Quick focus!! Happy habits – things we can do!
The students are asked at the outset to almost reap on a series of happy habits which they can engage in to promote well-being overall. These are the key tools and strategies and ways of being which, if they are formed into 'habits' can become truly life enhancing. The students are asked to identify what they do in each of the following key happiness building and habit forming areas:

GIVING – Do things for others
RELATING – Connect with people
EXERCISING – Take care of your body
APPRECIATING – Notice the world around
TRYING OUT- Keep learning new things
DIRECTION – Have goals to look forward to
RESILIENCE – Find ways to bounce back
EMOTION – Take a positive approach
ACCEPTANCE – Be comfortable with who you are
MEANING – Be part of something bigger

The habit of using CBT skills information sheet (1)
The next three activities focus upon introducing CBT and some of the key and most helpful strategies which can be easily used by the students in this session and beyond. Once again, there is an expectation that they will make use of these strategies on a regular basis and can also make use of the daily diary format that they used for mindfulness approaches for the purposes of keeping a record of when they used reframing, for example and how useful they found it in terms of correcting negative patterns of thinking or behaviour.

The facilitator may wish to provide a brief introduction to the process and intervention at the outset here as follows: The process of CBT helps to support young people in reconsidering negative assumptions. It also allows them to *learn how* to change their self-perceptions in order to improve their mental and emotional state – this is the key aim of this kind of intervention. Changing negative thought patterns or opinions will ultimately help young people to become more able to control and change their behaviours, but this does take practise. This is why, as with any 'well-being habit', another key element of the approach is the requirement to learn, and to put into practise, the skills or strategies discussed in any session.

CBT information sheet (2): how do the links work?
The facilitator(s) can highlight how the CBT approach breaks the problems into smaller parts. This enables the student to see how they're connected and how they affect them. This follows a process of A, B, C as follows:

- **A**, or the **activating event**, is often referred to as the 'trigger' – the thing that causes you to engage in the negative thinking.

- **B** represents these negative **beliefs**, which can include thoughts, rules and demands, and the meanings the individual attaches to both external and internal events.
- **C** is the **consequences**, or emotions, and the behaviours and physical sensations accompanying these different emotions. It is important to highlight and discuss with the students how the way that they think about a problem can affect how they feel physically and emotionally. It can also alter what they do about it. This is why the key aim for CBT is to break the negative, viscous cycle that some students may find themselves in. For example, if you think that you will get your work wrong you feel angry, and then you don't give it a try in case it is wrong.

This activity provides students with some examples of these links whilst then asking them to ponder the following ideas and questions:

Statement: How you think about something will become true

- Is this true?
- Can we change the way we think?
- Can we handle our problems differently to change how we feel and what we do?
- Can we gain more CONTROL over what happens to us in our lives?

Information sheet controlling thoughts

This activity highlights the ways in which we can so easily listen to negative or inaccurate thoughts and presents a strategy for overcoming this behaviour by way of distraction. Distraction helps us to take our mind off the thought by basically drowning it out and doing something else. The student can discuss each of these strategies in turn and consider which they might use themselves and perhaps also discuss those that they might currently be using for this purpose. It is important to note that like managing stress, this can be very personal and what works for each individual may differ according to their own learning and sensory preferences.

Take home habit task

Keeping Things in Perspective – Replacing the Negative with the Positive!

In this activity the students are asked to practise the strategy of reframing. When we feel upset or under pressure we tend to view everything negatively and think in an extreme way – we only look at the 'bad' things and take things personally. We also tend to exaggerate the consequences of the situation and blame ourselves or others in an irrational way. NB. OUR BODIES will REACT to the way our MIND has INTERPRETED the situation! We need to get our MINDS to reject the negatives and replace these with the POSITIVES. The students are asked to have a go at replacing a series of negative thoughts with more effective positives which are also grounded in reality!

Plenary and evaluation

The students can finally focus upon the following series of questions:

- What have we learnt about happiness in this session?
- Have we increased our knowledge?
- Have we gained any further useful strategies or techniques?
- Did everyone feel supported and comfortable?
- What was the most useful?
- What was the least useful?
- How would you change or adapt this session to make it more engaging and useful for other students in the future?

Quick focus!!
Happy habits – things we can do!

GIVING   Do things for others

Caring about others is fundamental to our happiness. Helping other people is not only good for them and a great thing to do, it also makes us happier and healthier too. Giving also creates stronger connections between people and helps to build a happier society for everyone. And it's not all about money – we can also give our time, ideas and energy. So if you want to feel good, do good!

Q: What do you do to help others?

RELATING   Connect with people

Relationships are the most important overall contributor to happiness. People with strong and broad social relationships are happier, healthier and live longer. Close relationships with family and friends provide love, meaning, support and increase our feelings of self-worth. Broader networks bring a sense of belonging. So taking action to strengthen our relationships and create new connections is essential for happiness.

Q: Who matters most to you?

EXERCISING   Take care of your body

Our body and mind are connected. Being active makes us happier as well as being good for our physical health. It instantly improves our mood and can even lift us out a depression. We don't all need to run marathons – there are simple things we can all do to be more active each day. We can also boost our well-being by unplugging from technology, getting outside and making sure we get enough sleep!

Q: How do you stay active and healthy?

APPRECIATING   Notice the world around

Ever felt there must be more to life? Well good news there is! And it's right here in front of us. We just need to stop and take notice. Learning to be more mindful and aware can do wonders for our well-being in all areas of life – like our walk to work, the way we eat or our relationships. It helps us get in tune with our feelings and stops us dwelling on the past or worrying about the future – so we get more out of the day-to-day.

Q: When do you stop and take notice?

TRYING OUT   Keep learning new things

Learning affects our well-being in lots of positive ways. It exposes us to new ideas and helps us stay curious and engaged. It also gives us a sense of accomplishment and helps boost our self-confidence and resilience. There are many ways to learn new things – not just through formal qualifications. We can share a skill with friends, join a club, learn to sing, play a new sport and so much more.

Q: What new things have you tried recently?

DIRECTION **Have goals to look forward to**

Feeling good about the future is important for our happiness. We all need goals to motivate us and these need to be challenging enough to excite us, but also achievable. If we try to attempt the impossible this brings unnecessary stress. Choosing ambitious but realistic goals gives our lives direction and brings a sense of accomplishment and satisfaction when we achieve them.

> **Q: What are your most important goals?**

RESILIENCE **Find ways to bounce back**

All of us have times of stress, loss, failure or trauma in our lives. But how we respond to these has a big impact on our well-being. We often cannot choose what happens to us, but in principle we can choose our own attitude to what happens. In practise it's not always easy, but one of the most exciting findings from recent research is that resilience, like many other life skills, can be learned.

> **Q: How do you bounce back in tough times?**

EMOTION **Take a positive approach**

Positive emotions – like joy, gratitude, contentment, inspiration and pride – are not just great at the time. Recent research shows that regularly experiencing them creates an 'upward spiral', helping to build our resources. So although we need to be realistic about life's up and downs, it helps to focus on the good aspects of any situation – the glass half full rather than the glass half empty.

> **Q: What are you feeling good about?**

ACCEPTANCE   **Be comfortable with who you are**

No one's perfect but so often we compare our insides to other people's outsides. Dwelling on our flaws – what we're not rather than what we've got – makes it much harder to be happy. Learning to accept ourselves, warts and all, and being kinder to ourselves when things go wrong, increases our enjoyment of life, our resilience and our well-being. It also helps us accept others as they are.

> **Q: What is the real you like?**

MEANING   **Be part of something bigger**

People who have meaning and purpose in their lives are happier, feel more in control and get more out of what they do. They also experience less stress, anxiety and depression. But where do we find 'meaning and purpose'? It might be our religious faith, being a parent or doing a job that makes a difference. The answers vary for each of us but they all involve being connected to something bigger than ourselves.

> **Q: What gives your life meaning?**

The habit of using CBT skills

Information Sheet (1)

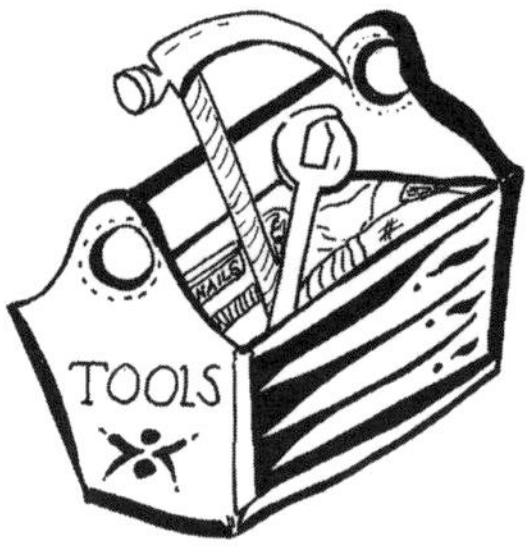

A set of tools to help you deal with problems and find the best solutions.

Looking at Links......

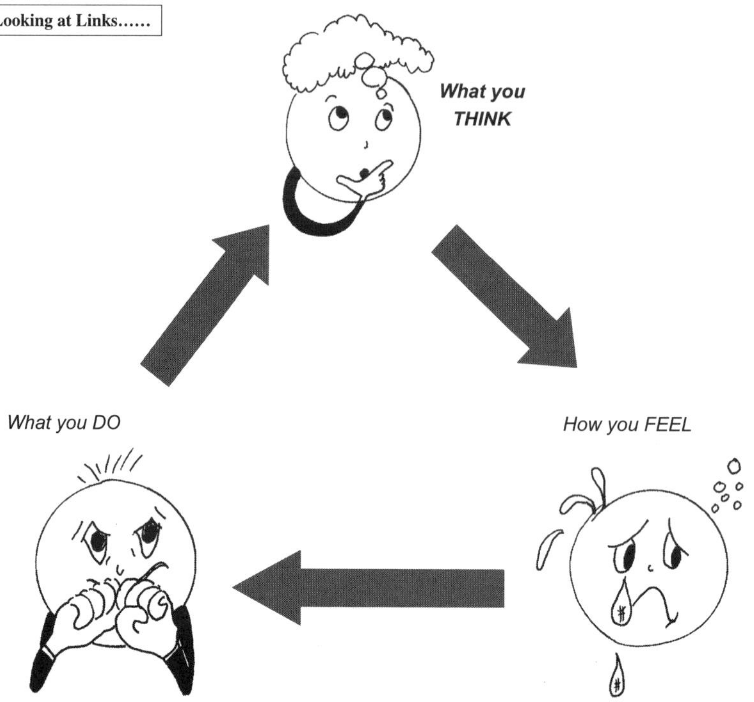

What you THINK

What you DO

How you FEEL

CBT Information Sheet (2)

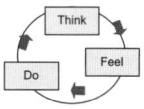 **HOW do the LINKS work?**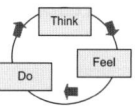

Some examples:

Think... ➡	Feel... ➡	Do... ➡
I'm useless at meeting new people	I feel scared and nervous when I meet new people	I don't talk to them and go quiet
No one in my form likes me	I feel sad and angry	I avoid going out at break and start to bunk off school
I'm rubbish at Maths	I feel dumb and fed up	I stop trying because I know I'll get it all wrong

Statement: How you think about something will become true

STOP, THINK & REFLECT

- Is this true?
- Can we change the way we think?
- Can we handle our problems differently to change how we feel and what we do?
- Can we gain more CONTROL over what happens to us in our lives?

Information sheet

Controlling thoughts

Facts

- We listen to our thoughts a lot
- We often accept negative thoughts as 'the truth' without really challenging them
- These thoughts can become louder and it becomes harder to hear the positive thoughts
- The more we listen to them, the more uncomfortable and down we fell and the less we do – it's a TRAP!!

The solution: distraction

- Helps you take your mind off the negative thoughts
- Helps you take CONTROL of your thoughts by thinking of something else
- You DROWN OUT those negative thoughts by ensuring your mind does what YOU want it to!

Strategies to try

- Describing what you see
- Puzzle it out!
- Get absorbed
- Self-talking
- Top talk
- Worry box
- Turn it down!
- Test it!
- Bin them!

Take home habit task

Keeping things in perspective
Replacing the negative with the positive!

When we feel upset or under pressure we tend to view everything negatively and think in an extreme way – we only look at the 'bad' things and take things personally. We also tend to exaggerate the consequences of the situation and blame ourselves or others in an irrational way.

NB: OUR BODIES will REACT to the way our MIND has INTERPRETED the situation!

We need to get our MINDS to reject the negatives and replace these with the POSITIVES. Have a go at replacing these negative thoughts (the first one is done for you to prompt you!):

Negative	Positive		
It runs in the family – my Mum was just like me!	This doesn't mean I have to be like her – I can change this behaviour!	Everything has to be absolutely perfect.	
Nobody likes me		Life is just unbearable	
I'll never pass that exam		I am so ugly – no one will fancy me	
I'm not good at anything		Things will never get better for me	
I always spoil everything		My work is never really good	

Session 7

The confidence and flow habits

Introduction and aims

In this session the students are asked to consider how using and practising the confidence and flow habits which can reinforce the feelings of positivity and overall well-being by ensuring that we again reduce the extent to which we engage in negative thinking. The focus is in using such tools and experiences and increasing them both in our daily lives in order to then preempt and reduce the level of negative automatic thinking that we may engage in on a daily basis. Again, such a focus can also empower us to live more productive and less anxiety filled lives. The students are introduced to the concepts of flow and confidence building in terms of their importance for maintaining mental/emotional health and well-being and the importance of recognising how and when these strategies can be helpfully employed – getting into the confidence and flow habits! The aims are as follows:

- To highlight the importance of adopting a positive outlook and experiencing flow on a regular basis in order to promote a sense of purpose, meaning and overall well-being
- To reinforce the need for students to choose to build these strengths in order to maintain a sense of well-being
- For students to be able to feel empowered to recognise, celebrate and effectively use these strategies whilst also recognising areas for development here
- To reinforce the skills of self-reflection, self-awareness and appropriate analysis of information.

At the start of this session, the facilitator can request feedback on the Take Home Habit Task, asking students how useful/otherwise they found this activity.

Icebreaker

This circle-time activity requires each member of the group to make a statement about themselves, which reveals something most of the group probably will not know. The facilitator should instruct group that the statements need to be kept positive (e.g., I am good at singing, or I am a member of the borough athletics team). It will be important for the facilitator to give some initial guidelines for this activity. For example, nobody is to comment after a member of this group has shared their information. Once the whole group has responded, the facilitator may wish to end the activity by summarising some of the talents within the group and pointing out that we are all different in some way and it is okay to 'be different' and that we need to be confident about our talents and our differences.

Strategy sheets

Get the flow habit

Csikszentmihalyi identified the concept of Flow in the 1960s when he was doing research into the creative process. He noticed how ARTISTS would ignore hunger, discomfort and tiredness when they were working on their paintings. They were 'IN THE FLOW' The students are asked simply: What are your 'flow' activities?

It may be useful to begin this individually and then to ask the students to feedback to the group as a whole and this will, in turn, highlight some of the similarities and differences in their responses.

The confidence habit! Using sources of confidence – what is confidence?

The students are asked to scale the definitions as follows: 1 = this is not me 3 = this is sometimes me 5 = this is always me

The idea here is to provide a rough assessment of their confidence levels and to highlight any areas that they may feel they need to develop further. This is quite a personal reflection and it may well be the case that some students may not wish to share this with others and this needs to be respected. What is important, is for the facilitator to stress that we all have a crisis of confidence at various points in our lives and how learning to build ourselves up and surrounding ourselves with people who can and do support us in the process is the habit we need to develop.

Four sources of confidence

This handout presents the students with the four main sources of confidence as follows:

1. EXPERIENCE
    Previous success will make you feel confident
2. ROLE MODELS
    Positive people who are confident will inspire you
3. ENCOURAGEMENT
    People who believe in you will make you feel confident
4. MANAGING FEELINGS
    This activity helps them to see that your ability to manage stress and cope when it goes wrong will help you to feel confident and that people, places, situations and memories can all give and take away our confidence. The students are asked to consider and then record their own examples of each category on the format provided.

Confidence givers and confidence takers

This activity reinforces the need for us to try to surround ourselves with those who are confidence givers and not confidence takers. The students are asked to identify these people in their lives. They will need to be careful in this activity in terms of identifying people within their closer family network and whether or not they want to share this with others. There will be times when student may disclose that someone very close to them is a confidence taker and that the relationship is not particularly good. This is when the facilitator(s) may provide some additional 1:1 support subsequent to the session in order to support the student in problem solving and finding a way forward with the situation. This may also require a referral to an outside agency if deemed appropriate.

Take home habit task

Recording my uniqueness – this is me! A happy habit!

The take home habit task reinforces the uniqueness of each individual, asking them to identify specific characteristics. This is a very healthy habit to get into and will hopefully enable the students to look out for the positives and affirm these on a daily basis rather than simply recognise what is negative or 'wrong' about them!

Plenary and evaluation

The students can finally focus upon the following series of questions:

- What have we learnt about happiness in this session?
- Have we increased our knowledge?
- Have we gained any further useful strategies or techniques?
- Did everyone feel supported and comfortable?
- What was the most useful?
- What was the least useful?
- How would you change or adapt this session to make it more engaging and useful for other students in the future?

Get the flow habit

Csikszentmihalyi identified the concept of Flow in the 1960s when he was doing research into the creative process.

He noticed how ARTISTS would ignore hunger, discomfort and tiredness when they were working on their paintings. They were 'IN THE FLOW'.

What are your 'flow' activities?

The confidence habit!

Using sources of confidence – what is confidence?

Scale the definitions

1 = this is not me	3 = this is some- times me			5 = this is always me	
You feel relaxed	1	2	3	4	5
You feel secure	1	2	3	4	5
You believe in yourself	1	2	3	4	5
You don't think others are always better than you	1	2	3	4	5
You set realistic goals	1	2	3	4	5
You do as well as you can	1	2	3	4	5
You don't believe in an aggressive way/show off when you feel insecure	1	2	3	4	5
You act confident even if you don't feel like it	1	2	3	4	5
Your self-esteem levels let you make mistakes and learn from them	1	2	3	4	5
You don't always worry about what others think	1	2	3	4	5
You tend to achieve what you want	1	2	3	4	5

Four sources of confidence

1. EXPERIENCE **Previous success will make you feel confident**	**2. ROLE MODELS** **Positive people who are confident will inspire you**
3. ENCOURAGEMENT **People who believe in you will make you feel confident**	**4. MANAGING FEELINGS** **Your ability to manage stress and cope when it goes wrong will help you to feel confident**

People, places, situations and memories can all give and take away our confidence. Record your example.

CONFIDENCE GIVERS	CONFIDENCE TAKERS

Stop, think and reflect

How can you reduce the number of confidence takers in your life?

What can you do? Draw up a list of strategies to avoid the confidence takers.

This will help to build your levels of happiness! Get into the habit of surrounding yourself with those confidence givers!

Take home habit task

Recording my uniqueness – this is me!

A Happy Habit!

I like myself
Because…

I like myself
Because…

I like myself
Because…

I like myself
Because…

Accept and
Respect Yourself

I like myself
Because…

I like myself
Because…

I like myself
Because…

I like myself
Because…

Signed _____   Date _____

Session 8

The visualisation and mastery habits

Introduction and aims

In this session the students are asked to consider how using and practising the visualisation and mastery habits which can reinforce the feelings of positivity and overall well-being by ensuring that we again reduce the extent to which we engage in negative thinking. The focus is in using such tools and experiences and increasing them both in our daily lives in order to then preempt and reduce the level of negative automatic thinking that we may engage in on a daily basis. Again, such a focus can also empower us to live more productive and less anxiety-filled lives. The students are introduced to the concepts of mastery and visualisation building in terms of their importance for maintaining mental/emotional health and well-being and the importance of recognising how and when these strategies can be helpfully employed – getting into the confidence and flow habits! The aims are as follows:

- To highlight the importance of adopting a positive outlook and experiencing mastery and engaging in positive and calming visualisation activities on a regular basis in order to promote a sense of purpose, meaning and overall well-being
- To reinforce the need for students to choose to build these strengths in order to maintain a sense of well-being
- For students to be able to feel empowered to recognise, celebrate and effectively use these strategies whilst also recognising areas for development here
- To reinforce the skills of self-reflection, self-awareness and appropriate analysis of information.

At the start of this session, the facilitator can request feedback on the Take Home Habit Task, asking students how useful/otherwise they found this activity.

Icebreaker

The facilitator should divide the students into pairs. Each student describes to their partner a 'sparkling moment' they have had. This is a moment when something has gone really well for them. This may be at school or home whilst spending time with friends. They should spend no more than three minutes describing their sparkling moment and should focus on:

- What made it a sparkling moment for them?

- How did they feel when they had their sparkling moment?
- Who else might have noticed?

Strategy sheets

Information sheet pleasure and mastery

In this activity the students are presented with the concepts of pleasure and mastery and the importance of developing both in our lives. The students are asked to read the following information: It can be useful to think of the amount of pleasure and mastery that good times give you. This is especially true if you have been feeling down. PLEASURE means the amount that you enjoy doing something. MASTERY means the amount of satisfaction that you get from the challenge of doing something. The amount of pleasure or mastery that you get from anything is a matter of personal opinion. You can judge the amount of pleasure that you get from doing something fun by using our pleasure-ometer. You can judge the amount of mastery that you get from doing something fun by using our mastery-ometer.

They are then required to use the two scales (pleasure- and mastery-ometers) in order to measure pleasure and mastery levels form a range of activities that they currently engage in. these might include musical, sporting or creative or technical activities.

Setting my goals – a good habit!

In this activity the students are asked to identify a series of personal goals for themselves and to then formulate or identify a priority goal. They are then asked to go through the following process in order to most effectively formulate this:

Think about your Priority Goal and ask yourself:

1. On a scale of 1 to 10 how much good will come if you achieve this goal and everything turns out well?
2. On a scale of 1 to 10 how much will your life be affected if you don't achieve this goal or things do not turn out well?

Think about it:

- If your answer to 1 is bigger than your answer to 2 it is clear you should go for it.
- If your answer to 2 is bigger than your answer to 1 think about a different goal.
- If your answers to 1 and 2 are the same think about how you can increase the upside. Then just do it.
- If you can't think of an upside don't do anything and think about the goal again tomorrow.

The idea here is to ensure that this goal REALLY is a priority!

Self-reflection activity – visualising the future

This self-reflection activity asks the students to identify 'the things I am going to do to make my dreams and ambitions for the future come true . . .'

The idea here is not simply to visualise the future but to also be specific about how we can make our dreams a reality by clearly identifying what we need to practically do in order to get there.

Take home habit task

Climb the mountain

Write or draw all your goals/things you would like to do on a piece of paper. Cut them out and then arrange them on the mountain below. Place the ones that seem easiest to achieve at the bottom, the most difficult at the top and the slightly easier ones in the middle. NEXT – start with the first and easiest task – when you've achieved it, climb a little further up the mountain and try the next one. Remember – take SMALL steps to reach the TOP!

Plenary and evaluation

The students can finally focus upon the following series of questions:

- What have we learnt about happiness in this session?
- Have we increased our knowledge?
- Have we gained any further useful strategies or techniques?
- Did everyone feel supported and comfortable?
- What was the most useful?
- What was the least useful?
- How would you change or adapt this session to make it more engaging and useful for other students in the future?

Information sheet

Pleasure and Mastery

It can be useful to think of the amount of pleasure and mastery that good times give you. This is especially true if you have been feeling down.

PLEASURE means the amount that you enjoy doing something.

MASTERY means the amount of satisfaction that you get from the challenge of doing something.

The amount of pleasure or mastery that you get from anything is a matter of personal opinion. You can judge the amount of pleasure that you get from doing something fun by using our pleasure-ometer. You can judge the amount of mastery that you get from doing something fun by using our mastery-ometer.

Pleasure-ometer

10 Maximum Pleasure!!!

9 Loads of
8 Pleasure

7
6 Medium
5 Pleasure
4

3 Mild
2 Pleasure

1 Minimum Pleasure

Pleasure and mastery

Mastery-ometer

10 Maximum Mastery!!!

9 Loads of
8 Mastery

7
6 Medium
5 Mastery
4

3 Mild
2 Mastery

1 Minimum Mastery

Use a daily diary format to plan as many good times as possible over the next week.

At the end of every day rate each of your good times on our pleasure-ometer and mastery-ometer.

Self-reflection activity

Visualising the future
These are the things I am going to do to make my dreams and ambitions for the future come true . . .

1.

2.

3.

4.

These are the things I would like other people to do to help me to make my dreams and ambitions for the future come true . . .

1.

2.

3.

4.

Setting my goals – a good habit!

My Friendship Goal

My Education Goal

My Career Goal

My Leisure Goal

My Health Goal

My Priority Goal is

Think about your Priority Goal and ask yourself:

3. On a scale of 1 to 10 how much good will come if you achieve this goal and everything turns out well?
4. On a scale of 1 to 10 how much will your life be affected if you don't achieve this goal or things do not turn out well?

Think about it:

- If your answer to 1 is bigger than your answer to 2 it is clear you should go for it.
- If your answer to 2 is bigger than your answer to 1 think about a different goal.
- If your answers to 1 and 2 are the same think about how you can increase the upside. Then just do it.
- If you can't think of an upside don't do anything and think about the goal again tomorrow.
- **Take home habit task**

Climb the mountain

Write or draw all your goals/things you would like to do on a piece of paper. Cut them out and then arrange them on the mountain below. Place the ones that seem easiest to achieve at the bottom, the most difficult at the top and the slightly easier ones in the middle. NEXT – start with the first and easiest task – when you've achieved it, climb a little further up the mountain and try the next one. Remember – take SMALL steps to reach the TOP!

Hardest

Easiest

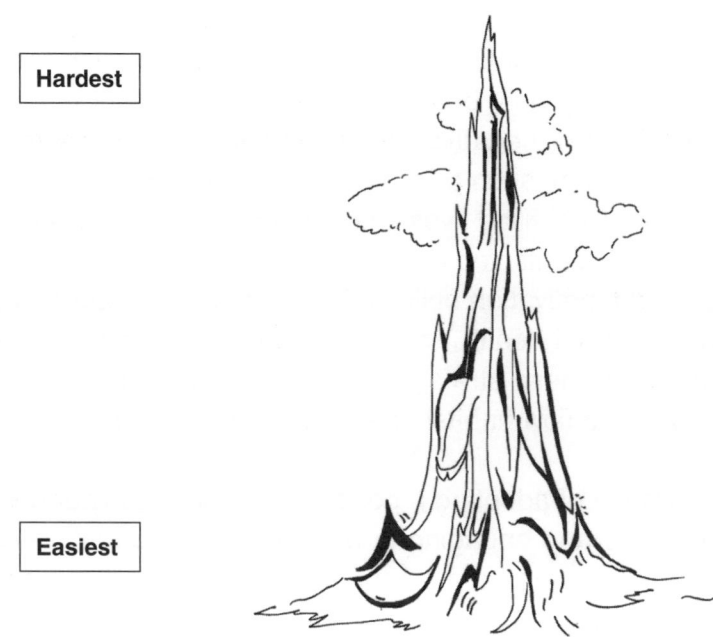

Session 9

Savouring and motivation habits

Introduction and aims

In this session the students are asked to consider how using and practising the savouring and motivation habits which can reinforce the feelings of positivity and overall well-being by ensuring that we again reduce the extent to which we engage in negative thinking. The focus is in using such tools and experiences and increasing them both in our daily lives in order to then preempt and reduce the level of negative automatic thinking that we may engage in on a daily basis. Again, such a focus can also empower us to live more productive and less-anxiety filled lives. The students are introduced to the concepts of savouring moments, feelings and experience and engaging in motivational practises and motivation building in terms of their importance for maintaining mental/emotional health and well-being and the importance of recognising how and when these strategies can be helpfully employed – getting into the confidence and flow habits! The aims are as follows:

- To highlight the importance of adopting a positive outlook and experiencing the savouring process and engaging in positive motivation activities on a regular basis in order to promote a sense of purpose, meaning and overall well-being
- To reinforce the need for students to choose to build these strengths in order to maintain a sense of well-being
- For students to be able to feel empowered to recognise, celebrate and effectively use these strategies whilst also recognising areas for development here
- To reinforce the skills of self-reflection, self-awareness and appropriate analysis of information.

At the start of this session, the facilitator can request feedback on the Take Home Habit Task, asking students how useful/otherwise they found this activity.

Icebreaker

This is a circle-time type activity. If space permits, it is preferable to have the students sit in a large circle in the room. It can also, however, be carried out at the students desks. It would be beneficial, however, for the facilitator to mix up friendship groups so that students are sitting next to somebody they do not know as well.

The students a given just a few minutes to discuss with each other and try to find three things they have in common in terms of ways they keep positive.

e.g., we both use positive reframing, we use mindfulness, we use relaxation, we help others, etc. Led by the facilitator, each pair then feeds back to the whole group and each participant should be encouraged to speak. The facilitator may conclude by summarising any key themes and identify any similarities and differences.

Strategy sheets

Motivate yourself! You are unique! Celebrate the difference!

In this activity the students are once again asked to celebrate their own uniqueness. They are reminded with the following motivational instructions: In all the world there is nobody quite like you! There are people who are different and people who are similar but nobody is exactly the same, with the same thoughts, ideas, feelings, behaviours, dreams, words, hopes, fantasies and appearance. They are asked to stop for a time and reflect upon these areas and to then jot down some notes in each box. It may be useful for students to share their information with a partner who could also then possibly contribute their views as to what makes this individual so unique.

Savouring habits! Savouring situations

The students are next introduced to the habit of savouring. What is savouring? Bryant and Veroff (2007) define savouring as any thoughts or behaviours capable of 'generating, intensifying and prolonging enjoyment'. Martin Seligman (2003) says that the ability to savour the positive experiences we have is one of the most important elements of happiness. Savouring situations fosters positive emotions and increases our overall well-being. The students are provided with a series of Questions to Consider as follows:

What are your most enjoyable activities?
How frequently do you STOP AND SAVOUR these experiences?
How do you savour these activities?
When do you savour these activities?
What presents you from savouring?
Why do we sometimes just 'rush through' an activity such as eating?
Why do we not take the time to simply stop and take in our surroundings?
Why do you think we have to make 'savouring' a deliberate act?
Once they have completed these on an individual basis it may also be useful for students to share their ideas ad thoughts via a whole group feedback session in which the facilitator(s) may act as a scribe and highlight any similarities and differences.

Savouring tenses!

In this activity the students are asked to think about and record the things they have savoured in the past, things they can savour now and things that they can savour in the future. They can record these on the chart provided and then get into the habit of SAVOURING!

Take home habit task

A motivational reflection

In this take home habit task, the students are asked to look into a mirror and draw what they can see – in effect, draw a self-portrait. They are the required to stop and think in order to reflect upon themselves, their achievements and the skills that they have learnt to date. Ideas can be recorded inside mirror frame on the format provided.

Plenary and evaluation

The students can finally focus upon the following series of questions:

- What have we learnt about happiness in this session?
- Have we increased our knowledge?
- Have we gained any further useful strategies or techniques?
- Did everyone feel supported and comfortable?
- What was the most useful?
- What was the least useful?
- How would you change or adapt this session to make it more engaging and useful for other students in the future?

Motivate yourself!

You are unique! Celebrate the difference!

In all the world there is nobody quite like you! There are people who are different and people who are similar but nobody is exactly the same, with the same thoughts, ideas, feelings, behaviours, dreams, words, hopes, fantasies and appearance. Stop for a time and reflect upon these areas – jot down some notes in each box.

A unique thought	A unique feeling	A unique fear

A unique hope	A unique fantasy	A unique dream

A unique appearance	A unique word or statement	A unique idea

There may be some things that you'd like to change in the future. Try to identify one or two of these and then work out how you might effect such a change and who will help and support you in doing this.

Savouring habits! Savouring situations

What is savouring? Bryant and Veroff (2007) define savouring as any thoughts or behaviours capable of 'generating, intensifying and prolonging enjoyment'.

Martin Seligman (2003) says that the ability to savour the positive experiences we have is one of the most important elements of happiness. Savouring situations fosters positive emotions and increases our overall well-being.

Questions to consider

What are your most enjoyable activities?

How frequently do you STOP AND SAVOUR these experiences?

How do you savour these activities?

When do you savour these activities?

What presents you from savouring?

Why do we sometimes just 'rush through' an activity such as eating?

Why do we not take the time to simply stop and take in our surroundings?

Why do you think we have to make 'savouring' a deliberate act?

Savouring tenses!

Think about and record the things you have savoured in the past, things you can savour now and things that you can savour in the future. Record these on the chart below and then SAVOUR!

Things I can savour from the PAST	Things I can savour NOW	Things I can savour in the FUTURE
e.g., holidays, time spent with friends/family, early childhood, etc.	e.g., friends, food, books, movies, hobbies etc.	e.g., career, relationships, friends, holidays, exam/ work success, etc.

A motivational reflection

Look into a mirror and draw what you see. Then stop and think! Reflect upon yourself, your achievements and the skills that you have learnt to date. Record your ideas inside a drawing of a mirror.

Skills   **Skills**

Achievements   **Achievements**

Now consider one achievement in detail and answer the following questions on the reverse of this sheet:

- Why did you achieve this?
- What did you feel, think and do at the time?
- Would you do anything differently in a similar situation in the future?

Session 10

A friendly future habit

Introduction and aims

In this session the students are asked to consider how using and practising a range of friendly habits which can reinforce the feelings of positivity and overall well-being by ensuring that we again reduce the extent to which we engage in negative thinking. The focus is in using such tools and habits and increasing their use in our daily lives in order to then preempt and reduce the level of negative automatic thinking that we may engage in and increase the quality of our relationships with others. Again, such a focus can also empower us to live more productive and less anxiety-filled lives. The students are introduced to the concepts of joint problem solving with others, reflecting upon the positive qualities of friends and engaging in and recording acts of kindness – again, the focus being on others rather than ourselves. This reinforces again the use of such happy habits in terms of maintaining mental/emotional health and well-being and the importance of recognising how and when these strategies can be helpfully employed – getting into and growing friendly habits! The aims are as follows:

- To highlight the importance of developing friendly habits and being outward focused and engaging in acts of kindness on a regular basis in order to promote a sense of purpose, meaning and overall well-being
- To reinforce the need for students to choose to build these strengths in order to maintain a sense of well-being
- For students to be able to feel empowered to recognise, celebrate and effectively use these strategies whilst also recognising areas for development here
- To reinforce the skills of self-reflection, self-awareness and appropriate analysis of information
- To reinforce the key concepts covered in the programme and celebrate the learning and developments that the students have undertaken to date.

At the start of this session, the facilitator can request feedback on the Take Home Habit Task, asking students how useful/otherwise they found this activity.

Icebreaker

In this activity the students are asked to brainstorm the question 'what is a true friend?' This activity reinforces the notion of friends as providers of emotional and practical support in times of stress. Students are encouraged to work in a pair or smaller group in order to pool their ideas which may well include some of the following definitions:

- someone who doesn't let you down
- someone who can keep your secrets
- someone who tries to help you find solutions
- someone who loves you
- someone who wants the very best for you
- someone who will really listen
- someone who won't judge you if you've done something wrong
- someone who will tell you the truth
- someone who always tries to help you
- someone who can say they are sorry or admit they are wrong
- someone who accepts you as you are
- someone who will share their feelings and plans with you.

Students can feedback their responses to the whole group and these could be recorded by the facilitator either on a flipchart / larger sheet of paper. It may be useful to highlight any agreements or disagreements as to what constitutes a 'true' friend and to also consider the possibility (or otherwise) of any friend achieving a state of perfection! Being a 'true' friend may be more to do with trying to do the best that you can and being able to admit to defeat or mistakes. Attempting perfection or expecting perfection can themselves be a cause of stress and unhappiness for many of us.

Strategy sheets

Friendship issues cards

One key element to being a good friend is the way in which we help and support others and engage actively in the problem solving process with them. This series of cards presents a range of problems experienced by young people. It would be useful to group students into pairs or smaller groups so that they can discuss each in turn and jointly formulate response/solution for the student facing each problem. This reinforces problem solving and empathy – the latter is clearly a habit that we should all develop and continually work at in order to maintain and further foster positive relationships with others and our own sense of being worthwhile and helpful in the social context.

Message in a bottle

In this activity the students are asked to write a note to a friend to support them in developing their skills and abilities. They can do this by telling the friend about how they themselves developed a talent or ability and overcame problems, developing a skill that they were previously bad at. The idea here is to reinforce the notion of 'true grit' and of persevering even when things seem like hard work and difficult to achieve. If we are persistent and keep trying to improve our skills we generally will be able to achieve some progress and it is therefore vital that we see mistakes s learning opportunities rather than the prompt to simply give up! This is probably one of the best habits that we can all develop and should all make use of on a regular basis if we want increase our levels of resilience and well-being.

Acts of kindness

Doing things to help others is not only good for the recipients – it has a positive payback for our happiness and health too. When people experience kindness it also makes them kinder as a result – so kindness is contagious! As the saying goes: 'if you want to feel good, do good.' Ultimately, this is common sense and a simple truth. The students are therefore encouraged in this activity to perform an extra act of kindness each day. This could be a compliment, a helping hand, a hug, a gift or something else. The act may be large or small and the recipient may not even be aware of it. Ideally these acts of kindness should be beyond the kind things we already do on a regular basis. And, of course, the acts mustn't put either party in danger! The students are asked to do at least one extra kind act each day for a week, ideally a different one each day. The activity sheet provides a range of ideas for different acts of kindness but of course the students are free to devise their own! Initially they are asked to tick against those on the list that they may already have done at some point.

Random acts of kindness diary

In this activity the students are asked to perform at least one kind act each day for a week, ideally a different one each day. Ideally this random act of kindness should be something beyond the kind things that the student might do on a regular basis. They can make use of the sheet to keep a record of their acts of kindness. They can also note down how they felt about doing them and whether they found them easy or difficult to complete.

Take home habit task

The final activity involves rewarding students who have participated with a certificate of attendance and achievement. These can be pre prepared and laminated as appropriate in order to make a special event of this last session.

Plenary and evaluation

The students can finally focus upon the following series of questions:

- What have we learnt about happiness in this session?
- Have we increased our knowledge?
- Have we gained any further useful strategies or techniques?
- Did everyone feel supported and comfortable?
- What was the most useful?

- What was the least useful?
- What have we learnt during the programme as a whole about how to use happy habits? It may be helpful to quickly reinforce the main aims of the programme in order to refresh the student's memories and also to provide a measure against which they can judge the extent to which these may or may not have been met. The facilitator may wish to record the following on a white board/flip chart for this purpose:

    1. *To provide students with a confidential and supportive framework in which they can begin to reflect upon their feelings, behaviours, actions and happiness levels.*
    2. *To allow each student in the group to begin to understand the nature and causes of stress and anxiety both in themselves and others.*
    3. *To encourage students to distinguish between positive and negative responses to stress and anxiety.*
    4. *To encourage an understanding regarding the ways in which happy habits from positive psychology can support the maintenance and further development of well-being.*
    5. *To increase students' awareness regarding the fact that people will need different levels of support at different times in their lives.*
    6. *To encourage students to further develop empathy for others alongside their own problem solving skills within a supportive framework.*
    7. *To encourage students to consider and practise a range of strategies from CBT and Mindfulness approaches for coping with difficult feelings and events we may all encounter on a daily basis.*
    8. *To increase students' level of confidence in their own abilities to cope with stressful situations and conflicts in an assertive and positive way and to be able to bounce back and not give up when the going gets tough.*
    9. *To ensure that students are aware of their own strengths and the importance of continually building and using these throughout their lives.*
    10. *To understand and use the happy habits of engaging in flow activities, savouring the positives, and the need to develop friendly habits in order to show gratitude and sustain positive relationships over time.*

- How would you change or adapt this programme as a whole to make it more engaging and useful for other students in the future?

Friendship issues cards

Issue (1) Your friend can never compromise when you have an argument, he always has to 'win'.	**Issue (2)** Your friend thinks he's gay and has told you not to tell anyone else as he feels nervous about this.	**Issue (3)** Your friend's dad is always putting her down and making her feel stupid and thick.
Issue (4) Your friend recently lost his grandfather. He is feeling very down and rejecting support from friends.	**Issue (5)** Your friend has become more fundamentalist since 9/11 and now doesn't want to go around with non-Muslims.	**Issue (6)** Your friend's mum is a racist and won't have you in her house because you are black.
Issue (7) Your friend is drinking too much and having unprotected sex when she's drunk at parties.	**Issue (8)** Your friend is getting stressed about exams because he thinks he won't be able to pass any of them as he's not as clever as you.	**Issue (9)** Your friend thinks it's okay to two-time his girlfriend.
Issue (10) Your friend is really possessive and doesn't want you to have a close relationship with anyone else.	**Issue (11)** Your friend enjoys smoking cannabis but you don't.	**Issue (12)** Your friend makes jokes about people with disabilities. Your younger brother has cerebral palsy.
Issue (13) Your friend is always borrowing money from you and others and never pays it back.	**Issue (14)** Your friend always buys the same clothes as you and can't seem to develop her own individual style.	**Issue (15)** Your friend thinks girls are only good for sex and that they can't be good friends like boys.

Stop, think and reflect!

How would you solve these friendship issues? Work in small groups, share your ideas and agree on plans of action. Feedback to the whole group.

Message in a bottle

Write a note to a friend to support them in developing their skills and abilities.

Tell them about how you developed a talent or ability and overcame problems, developing a skill that you were previously bad at . . .

Send the message in a bottle!

Acts of kindness

Doing things to help others is not only good for the recipients – it has a positive payback for our happiness and health too. When people experience kindness it also makes them kinder as a result – so kindness is contagious!

As the saying goes: 'if you want to feel good, do good.'

Perform extra act of kindness each day

This could be a compliment, a helping hand, a hug, a gift or something else. The act may be large or small and the recipient may not even be aware of it.

Ideally your acts of kindness should be beyond the kind things you already do on a regular basis. And, of course, the acts mustn't put you or others in danger!

Do at least one extra kind act each day for a week, ideally a different one each day.

Here are some ideas for acts of kindness:

• Give up your seat	• Tell someone if you notice they're doing a good job
• Hold a door open for someone	• Pass on a book you've enjoyed
• Give a (sincere) compliment	• Say sorry (you know who to)
• Make someone laugh	• Forgive someone for what they've done
• Give someone a hug	• Visit a sick friend, relative or neighbour
• Take time to really listen to someone	• Buy an unexpected gift for someone
• Make someone new feel welcome	• Bake something for a neighbour
• Let one car in on every journey	• Pay for someone in the queue behind
• Give directions to someone who's lost	• Do a chore that you don't normally do
• Have a conversation with a stranger	• Help out someone in need
• Pick up litter as you walk	• Offer to look after a friend's children
• Let someone in front of you in the supermarket queue	• Offer to mow your neighbour's lawn
• Tell someone they mean a lot to you	• Donate your old things to charity
• Let someone have your parking spot	• Give food to a homeless person and take time to talk with them
• Read a story with a child	• Visit someone who may be lonely
• Offer your change to someone struggling to find the right amount	• Give blood
• Treat a loved one to breakfast in bed	• Get back in contact with someone you've lost touch with
• Buy cakes or fruit for your colleagues	• Organise a fundraising event
• Invite your neighbour round for a drink and a chat	• Volunteer your time for a charity
• Offer to help with someone's shopping	• Plan a street party

Tick against each of these acts you have already completed once in your life!

© 2015, *Using Positive Psychology to Enhance Student Achievement*, Tina Rae and Ruth MacConville, Routledge

Random acts of kindness diary

Do at least one kind act each day for a week, ideally a different one each day.

Ideally your random act of kindness should be something beyond the kind things you do on a regular basis.

Use this sheet to keep a record of your acts of kindness. You can also note down how you felt about doing them and whether you found them easy or difficult.

1. Day/date:

What did you do? Who for? How did it go?

2. Day/date:

What did you do? Who for? How did it go?

3. Day/date:

What did you do? Who for? How did it go?

4. Day/date:

What did you do? Who for? How did it go?

5. Day/date:

What did you do? Who for? How did it go?

6. Day/date:

What did you do? Who for? How did it go?

7. Day/date:

What did you do? Who for? How did it go?

Certificate of completion

Name

You have successfully completed the Happy Habits Course

Well done! You are a star!

Signed

Dated

Section 5
Guidance for parents

Parents and carers have a critical role to play in enabling their children to develop the behaviours and attitudes that are promoted by the programmes that are contained in Section 3 of this book. It is therefore important that steps are taken to ensure that parents are given opportunities to be involved in the work as early as possible.

Parents and carers are naturally highly invested in helping their children enjoy school, have friends and are doing well. They are therefore likely to be very reassured to know that specific steps are being taken in school to introduce children to the sorts of habits and behaviours that can enable their children to recognise and use their strengths. A number of steps can be taken to encourage parents and carers involvement and support for the programme.

Setting up a school meeting for parents

When setting up a meeting it will be important to:

- Send out a letter as early as possible to inform parents about the programme and to therefore allow them enough time to make plans to attend. In our experience, holding meetings during the early evening is likely to enable more parents to attend.
- In the letter, make it clear that if parents would like to discuss any aspect of the programme in advance of the meeting, they are welcome to contact a named person at the school. It will be helpful to provide specific times and ways (phone call, e-mail exchange, brief meeting) when this contact could take place. This offer is likely to reassure parents, and an initial personal contact can significantly increase parents confidence and willingness to be engaged in the programme. Initial contact can be an opportunity for parents to air any concerns that they may have and ask specific questions that may be difficult to raise in a group setting.
- Think about the location of the meeting. A large, public hall is not likely to provide a welcoming environment. If possible, select a small, comfortable, welcoming room.
- It will be important to keep the emphasis of the meeting positive. It will be helpful if parents have had an opportunity in advance of the meeting to be introduced to the results of their child's strengths assessment and also be invited to undertake the strengths assessment themselves.

- Throughout the meeting allow plenty of time for discussion and questions.
- Be aware that the meeting may raise particular issues for some parents and may therefore want to raise issues with you in confidence after the meeting.

Running the meeting

Introduction
It will be important to emphasise throughout the meeting that parents are the most influential people in a child's life and have a particular responsibility to encourage their child's strengths and reinforce the positive messages that are being emphasised throughout the programme.

Making the intangible tangible
We all know that families are crucial, and it is clearly important to emphasise that message to parents; however, it can be a sensitive message to convey without sounding patronising. It can also sound like an intangible message without what it actually means in practise. It is clear that the vast majority of families want to do right by their children even if they have had tough knocks in life. One of the ways that we can help them is by articulating key messages of what that means: what parents can actually do on a day-to-day basis.

It could therefore be helpful to introduce the meeting by referring to the five top findings of the most recent and broadest research into families, *American Family Assets Study* by Minneapolis' Search Institute (Syvertsen, Roehlkepartain, and Scales 2012), a non-profit organization dedicated to discovering what children and young people need to succeed. The Search Institute has spent 50 years looking into the strengths in young people lives, and in the last 25 years, the institute has focused on how to develop the assets that young people need to grow up successfully. Their study, which polled a diverse cross-section of more than 1,500 families, set out to understand the power of focusing on strengths and emphasising that as part of counterbalancing the negative messages about families that are out there. The results of the study centre around five common qualities or actions:

1. **Nurturing relationships:** The way we get along shapes family life. It matters. It's what gets us through challenging times. Do family members, listen and encourage each other? Asking each other about the highs and lows of the day is a great way to keep in emotional touch.
2. **Establish routines:** Create traditions, celebrate birthdays, half birthdays, have a family calendar that the whole family has access to. Family mealtimes are a secret weapon and the best tool to check in and get a barometer on how children and young people are doing.
3. **Maintain expectations:** Are rules fair and are boundaries clear? Can you talk about tough topics and is everyone contributing? Is your child moving towards being in charge of her/his life and contributing to the family? The key message as children grow is: you have a real role to play as you begin to contribute back to the family in adult ways.

4. **Adapt to challenges together**: Families go through tough times. It is important to adjust when things come up. Do you work together to solve problems? Is everybody's voice heard? It's actually something to celebrate that we can get through the tough time.
5. **Connect:** The best families are connected and engaged in the world. Are there nearby places each member of your family feels at home: with neighbours, at a local coffee shop, a gym, a church, in friends and families homes?

Suggest that if parents would like to know more about the programme they may wish find it on the web at: www.search/institute.org/research/family/-well-being

The PowerPoint presentation that is included in Section 2 of this book could be usefully adapted for parents and presented as the main focus of the session.

Follow-up suggestions

Suggest that parents:

- Talk to their child about the programme
  Inform parents that students will be encouraged to talk about what they have learnt in the sessions and share the folder of activities that they build up during the programme with adults at home.
- Do the activities
  Most people learn better by doing. The activities which form the main body of the programme is where the real learning happens. Suggest to parents that they do the activities themselves and be prepared to e-mail the activity sheets home if that is possible. Alternatively, all activity sheets may be photocopied.

End of the meeting

An important message at the end of the meeting will be to emphasise that parents are the most important role model in the young person's life and therefore have an important role to play in reinforcing the positive messages that students will be taught during the programme.

Thank parents for attending and wish them success and fun in supporting their child during the programme.

Example letter to parents

Dear

This term (year) we will be working on a programme which has been written to introduce your child to the key messages of positive psychology. The programme will focus on recognising and celebrating each student's strengths.

This programme will encourage students to recognise their individual qualities and characteristics and encourage them to build happy, healthy habits.

We will be encouraging your child to talk about what they have learnt in the sessions with you at home and also share with you the activities that they have completed.

It would be very helpful if you could take time to talk to your child about what they have learnt. You may wish to try out some of the activities yourself.

A meeting has been arranged for parents to learn more about the programme and have the opportunity to ask any questions about the sessions.

The meeting will take place on …….. at …………….. It will be held in room……… It is intended that the meeting will last for approximately 2 hours.

I look forward to seeing you at the meeting.

Yours sincerely,

References

Barnes, J. (ed.), 1984, *The Complete Works of Aristotle*, Vols. 1–2, Princeton, NJ: Princeton University Press.

Baumeister, R.F., 2005, *The Cultural Animal: Human nature, meaning and social life,* Oxford: Oxford University Press.

Boniwell, I., and Ryan, L., 2012, *Personal Well-Being Lessons for Secondary Schools: Positive psychology in action for 11 to 14 year olds,* Maidenhead: Open University Press.

Britton, K., 2008, Social contagion: spiral up or down? *Positive Psychology News Daily.* April 7, pp. 1–2.

Brooks, D., 2011, *The Social Animal: A story of how success happens,* London: Short Books.

Bryant, F.B., and Veroff, J., 2007, *Savoring: A new model of positive experience,* Mahwah, NJ: Lawrence Erlbaum Associates.

Clifton, D.O., and Anderson, C.E., 2002, *Now Discover Your Strengths: How to develop your strengths and those of people like you.* London: Pocket Books.

Dean, J., 2013, *Making Habits, Breaking Habits: How to make changes that stick,* London: OneWorld Publications.

Duckworth, A., and Seligman, M., 2005, Self-discipline outdoes IQ in predicting academic performance of adolescents, *Psychological Science*, 16: 939–44.

Duckworth, A.L., & Allred, K.M., (2007), Temperament in the classroom, in Shiner, R.L. & Zenter, M. (eds.), *Handbook of Temperament.* New York: Guildford Press.

Duckworth, A., Peterson, C., Matthews, M.D., and Kelly, D.R., 2007, Grit, perseverance, and passion for long-term goals, *Journal of Personality and Social Psychology,* 92(6): 1087–1101.

Duhigg, C., 2012, *The Power of Habit: Why we do what we do and how to change*, London: Random House Books.

Dutton, J., 2003, *Energize Your Workplace: How to create and sustain high-quality connections at work*, San Francisco: Jossey Bass.

Dweck, C.S., 2006, *Mindset: The new psychology of success*, New York: Ballantine Books.

Fox Eades, J., 2008, *Celebrating Strengths: Building strengths based schools*, Coventry: CAPP Press.

Frederickson, B., 2009, *Positivity*, New York: Crown Publishers.

Gable, S.L., Reis, H.T., Impett, E., and Asher, E.R., 2004, What do you do when things go right? The intrapersonal and interpersonal benefits of sharing positive events. *Journal of Personality and Social Psychology*, 87: 228–45.

Gardner, H., 2011, *Frames of Mind: The theory of multiple intelligences*, 10th ed. Philadelphia: Basic Books.

Goleman, D., 2007, *Social Intelligence: The new science of human relationships*, London: Arrow Books.

James, W., 1980, *Habit,* Classic Reprint Series, Forgotten Books. New York: Henry Holt & Co.

Jolly, M., and McNamara, E., 1991, Towards better behavior: Part 2 Assessment. Available from TBB, 7, Quinton Close, Ainsdale, Merseyside PR8 2TD.

Kaufman, S.B., 2013, *Ungifted Intelligence Redefined: The truth about talent, practice, creativity, and the many paths to greatness*, New York: Basic Books.

Kessler, D., A., 2009, *The end of overeating: Taking control of our insatiable appetite*, London, Penguin Books Ltd.

Kraemer, S., 1999, Promoting resilience: changing concepts of parenting and child care, *International Journal of Child and Family Welfare*, 3: 273–287.

Linley, A., 2008, *Average to A+; Realizing strengths in yourself and others*, Coventry: CAPP Press.

MacConville, R.M., and Rae, T., 2012, *Building Happiness, Resilience and Motivation in Adolescents: A positive psychology curriculum for well-being*, London: Jessica Kingsley Publishers.

Nettle, D., 2005, *Happiness; The science behind your smile*, Oxford: Open University Press.

Peterson, C., and Seligman, M., 2004, *Character Strengths and Virtues: A handbook and classification*, New York: Oxford University Press.

Seldon, A., 2011, Today, class we shall build your character; pupils must be taught personal skills if we want more to succeed. Think Tank, New Ideas for the 21st Century, *Times,* December 31, 2011.

Seligman, M., 2003, *Authentic Happiness: Using the new positive psychology to realize your potential for lasting fulfilment,* New York: Free Press.

Seligman, M., 2011, *Flourish: A new understanding of happiness and well-being and how to achieve them*, London: Nicholas Brearley Publishing.

Semple, R.J., and Lee, J., 2008, Treating anxiety with mindfulness: Mindfulness-based cognitive therapy for children, in Greco, L.A. & Hayes, S.C. (eds.), *Acceptance and Minfulness Treatments for Children and Adolescents: A practitioners guide,* Oakland: New Harbinger Publications.

Smith, I.K., 2010, *Happy: Simple steps to get the most out of life,* New York: St. Martin's Press.

Syvertsen, A.K., Roehlkepartain, E.C., and Scales, P.C., 2012, The American Family Assets Study, www.search/institute.org/research/family-well-being

Teasdale, J.D., Segal, Z., and Williams, V.A., 1995, How does cognitive therapy prevent depressive relapse and why should attentional control (mindfulness) training help? *Behavior research therapy,* 33(1): 25–39.

Tough, P., 2012, *How Children Succeed: Grit, curiosity, and the hidden power of character*, Boston: Houghton Mifflin Harcourt.

Ungar, M., 2006, *Strengths-based Counselling with At-risk Youth*, Thousand Oaks, CA: Corwin Press.

Wilson, T.D., 2011, *Redirect: The surprising new science of psychological change*, London: Allen Lane.

Yeager, J.M., Fisher, S.W., Shearon, D.N., 2011, *Smart Strengths: Building character, resilience and relationships in youth*, New York: Kravis Publishing.

Index